DARK PSYCHOLOGY SECRETS

Learn The Secrets Of The Mind And Control Your Life With Persuasion, Manipulation, And Emotional Intelligence

Marisa Leary

© Copyright 2020 by Marisa Leary. All right reserved.

The work contained herein has been produced with the intent to provide relevant knowledge and information on the topic on the topic described in the title for entertainment purposes only. While the author has gone to every extent to furnish up to date and true information, no claims can be made as to its accuracy or validity as the author has made no claims to be an expert on this topic. Notwithstanding, the reader is asked to do their own research and consult any subject matter experts they deem necessary to ensure the quality and accuracy of the material presented herein.

This statement is legally binding as deemed by the Committee of Publishers Association and the American Bar Association for the territory of the United States. Other jurisdictions may apply their own legal statutes. Any reproduction, transmission or copying of this material contained in this work without the express written consent of the copyright holder shall be deemed as a copyright violation as per the current legislation in force on the date of publishing and subsequent time thereafter. All additional works derived from this material may be claimed by the holder of this copyright.

The data, depictions, events, descriptions and all other information forthwith are considered to be true, fair and accurate unless the work is expressly described as a work of fiction. Regardless of the nature of this work, the Publisher is exempt from any responsibility of actions taken by the reader in conjunction with this work. The Publisher acknowledges that the reader acts of their own accord and releases the author and Publisher of any responsibility for the observance of tips, advice, counsel, strategies and techniques that may be offered in this volume.

TABLE OF CONTENTS

Introduction 1
Chapter 1 *What Is Dark Psychology?* 2
Chapter 2 *Characteristics Of Dark Psychology* 8
Chapter 3 *Dark Psychology Terms Explained* 16
Chapter 4 *Typical Tactics Of Dark Psychology* 24
Chapter 5 *Average People Engaging In Dark Psychology* 31
Chapter 6 *The Dark Side Of Dark Psychology* 39
Chapter 7 *Dark Psychology And Social Media* 46
Chapter 8 *Deviant Behavior And Dark Psychology* 53
Chapter 9 *Making Dark Psychology Work For You* 60
Conclusion 66
Description 67

INTRODUCTION

Congratulations on purchasing *Dark Psychology Secrets,* and thank you for choosing this book to begin your study of dark psychology.

This book is everything you need to get started on the path to understanding dark psychology. This book is designed to be user-friendly so that you move seamlessly from foundational concepts into the more complicated and nuanced aspects of this topic. You will learn how to take the basics and recognize them, understand where dark psychology can go too far, and develop the skills needed to apply it thoughtfully in your own life, if you dare. If you have ever wondered why success comes so easily to those in power, you will know by the end of this book. If you have ever wondered why victims fall prey so easily to well-known predators, you will know by the end of this book. And if you have ever wondered how to enjoy the kind of success enjoyed by the powerful elite, you will get the chance to taste that same success with just a little study and practice. This is your ultimate guide. The secrets are waiting in this book, just for you, and it is the author's sincere hope that you will finish the book satisfied that you are now an expert in the world of dark psychology.

There are plenty of books on dark psychology on the market, so thank you for trusting this one to be your guide. Every effort was made to ensure that it creates a lasting impact on your understanding and use of dark psychology practices. Please enjoy!

CHAPTER 1
What Is Dark Psychology?

You have begun your journey into dark psychology, and the most obvious first step is to understand what it is. The answer is both simple and complicated, so feel free to return to this opening chapter to remind yourself of the basic foundation of what dark psychology is. Grapple with the definition and use it as a way to challenge your understanding of the concept as this book delves deeper into its nuances.

Dark Psychology Basics

In its purest definition, dark psychology is the innate human ability to prey upon others, with or without a clear motivation. It acknowledges that within every human being is the capability to act upon these inclinations to victimize and engage in predatory behavior. This predatory behavior manifests itself as strategic manipulation and coercion that often goes unnoticed by the victim.

The most common form of dark psychology manifests itself as minor forms of aggression and behaviors. A reaction to a negative stimulus can cause an immediate desire to perform harm or to engage in violent retaliation. In other words, if someone has hurt you in some way, the thought may cross your mind to hit them. You don't necessarily act on the thought, but it's still there. This is entirely human. Everyone has the basic requirements of dark psychology within them.

This is also a uniquely human phenomenon because it strays from the basic instincts common to most other living things. Violence in the animal world serves the purpose of securing a territory, securing reproductive capabilities, or pure survival. Humans, on the other hand, can engage in not only physical violence but also emotional violence in order to inflict pain on someone. This can come from a large range of motivations outside of territory, reproduction, or survival, or it can have no motivation at all. This is why dark psychology requires careful study because it takes a look into a much darker side of the human condition.

When studying dark psychology, it is essential to anchor the idea that we are all capable of utilizing dark psychology, but the ways in which it is used vary from person to person. In other words, it falls along a spectrum that can range from only thoughts of predatory behavior to actualized predatory behavior that is incredibly violent and without a clear motive. So, in that sense, dark psychology is not necessarily inherently evil or even deplorable. It is a natural part of being human. The danger lies in where a person falls along this spectrum and whether their decisions can be connected to motivations or not.

Another part of understanding this topic is learning that dark psychology is in constant use. Whether you are conscious of it or not is different. For example, dark psychology has and always will play a role in advertising practices. At its heart, advertising is seeking to make consumers the "victims" of their sales tactics, even if what is being sold has no direct impact on someone's basic human needs. There is no evolutionary justification for why you may want a new phone, but dark psychology tactics can be used to convince you otherwise. Word choice, product placement, colors, and catchphrases can all be used to sway you to want a product regardless of its utility.

Now that you are beginning to understand the ubiquitous qualities of dark psychology, you may be in a panic. You may even be having regrets about a recent purchase you made or a response you gave to someone who used dark psychology to draw you in. Stop right there because it is not worth giving yourself a headache over what is done. Instead, take this moment as an opportunity to see that learning about dark psychology can also give you power over dark psychology. Rather than living in a world where you are unconsciously tempted into all manner of behaviors and decisions, you will now live in a world where you are self-aware and can combat the more deviant aspects of dark psychology.

Dark psychology divides itself very easily into two categories: the perpetrator and the victim. These two categories can be made up of individuals or multiple individuals, but both must be represented in order for dark psychology to be in action. The whole point is to gain control over another's behavior, so at least two people must be involved. The perpetrator is, of course, the person or people who are actively using dark psychological tactics. The perpetrator most often has one clear goal, and that is to satisfy something they want. They may want the victim to feel belittled, friendless, unsuccessful, or simply want them to be in physical pain. To secure what they want, they will use a variety of manipulation tactics to create the desired result. You will learn more about the specifics of these tactics in a future chapter, but for now, understand that there are recognizable tools used by perpetrators to get what they want from their victims. If successful, the perpetrator will have manipulated and coerced the victim into committing the desired behaviors or reactions. A successful perpetrator will often return to the same victim and fine-tune their tactics over time to master the art of dark psychology.

Another way to think of it is that the perpetrator is controlling your mind. They are observing you, watching for what makes you behave in certain ways, and then using those triggers to generate the desired response. It is calculating and specific. This is the characteristic of dark psychology that steps beyond the natural angry responses we may have and becomes a deeply intentional act that can stray into criminal and deviant behavior. The victim can be anyone, as long as the victim is the subject of the perpetrator's actions. The victim is most often unaware of how dark psychology is being used against them. They may not even see the perpetrator as someone "bad." Instead, they believe that their responses are born of their own free decisions. What they are unaware of is how everything they do and say is as the perpetrator predicted. The perpetrator is often masterful at making the victim feel that they chose the behavior rather than believing that they were manipulated. The victim may even defend and support the perpetrator if the perpetrator is strong enough in the tactics of dark psychology. This is where dark psychology becomes most dangerous because it is literally morphing the mind of the victim. It is not a relatively harmless sales strategy but is true mind control and manipulation.

Do not be entirely misled by the use of the word victim. It has a negative implication, but that does not mean it is always negative to be a victim or to be a perpetrator. It is inevitable that dark psychology tactics will be used on you and by you. What is most significant is the motivation. For example, you may have a friend you know is in the throes of an abusive relationship. It is entirely valid to use what you know about them and their personality to manipulate them into seeing the abuse they are suffering. While no one likes to engage in or be the victim of manipulation, there are relevant times to put dark psychology to use.

A Brief History of Dark Psychology

If you were to attempt to do some initial research on the history of dark psychology, you would come up with woefully few results. That is because most psychological experiments that deal with factors related to dark psychology will go by other names. Some common ones would be social psychology or social experiments. Below you will find two experiments that ventured into the realms of dark psychology as well as a psychologist who was a pioneer for the kinds of social experiments in use today. Studies and psychologists such as these provide another source of validation for the permeation and prevalence of dark psychology within humanity.

The first study of interest was performed by Stanley Milgram. In his study, subjects were told to sit at a panel, which had a microphone, speaker, and a labeled dial. They were to listen to a subject answer a series of questions. The subjects were at the panel, and the responders were supposedly in another room. Subjects were unable to see the responder, but they were able to hear all of their responses and other sounds over the speaker. The responders, of course, never received a shock but were simply recordings of a person's voice played for the subjects. Subjects were told the dial was to be used to deliver an electric shock to the responder if they gave an incorrect response to a question. The dial was labeled with varying degrees of pain inflicted, including the highest label of "fatal." The subjects who sat at the panel would deliver these shocks as directed by a person in the room with them. This person had a white lab coat on but did not present any other credentials. If the subject hesitated to increase the shock as the responder answered more questions incorrectly, the person in the white lab coat would follow a script of responses that all ultimately told the subject they had no choice and that it had to be done.

The results of this experiment were shocking, but they show very clearly the power of dark psychology at work. The subject who was told to deliver the shocks continued to increase the severity of pain, even to the "fatal" level, and even while hearing pre-recorded screams coming from the responder. Sixty-five percent of subjects did not stop at the "fatal" level, and even those who did refuse to continue simply left after the experience and in no way showed concern over the fate of the responder they were shocked.

What this experiment clearly illustrates is twofold. First, it validates that we are all capable of performing acts we may deem "immoral" or "wrong" in the right circumstances. Second, it illustrates the dangers of positions of authority. Although the person with the lab coat was unknown to the subject, the lab coat gave the wearer a kind of authority, which the subject responded to, even against their better judgment or moral values. Normal human beings were willing to engage in acts of torture because they trusted in that authority, even if it meant killing an unknown person. Dark psychology can be used to terrible effect when utilized by the wrong individuals, especially those entrusted with power.

The second experiment was designed by Philip Zimbardo and was called the Stanford Prison Experiment. The goal of the study was to perfectly simulate the conditions of prison. Subjects were divided into two groups, prison guards and inmates. They were given quarters that were designed to mimic a prison in every way possible, a true recreation of the prison environment. After that, the subjects were left to operate in their roles as they saw fit without any outside direction or interference. The study was designed to last for a two-week period, but it had to be shut down after only six days. Within those six days, the prison guards had already begun to engage in sadistic and manipulative ways towards the prisoners. Of course, no one expected that they would fall so easily into these patterns of behavior, and none wanted to acknowledge that the circumstances manipulated them into making decisions uncharacteristic of their personalities and personal morals.

This experiment is another prime example of dark psychology in action. All it took was the appropriate stimulus for individuals to engage in dangerous and exploitative behavior. The subjects entered as peers, but the labels they were given, one with innate authority and one without, meant that they changed as people. This experiment has a deeper implication that goes beyond an abuse of power. This study was a group study rather than an individual study. That means that, regardless of who initiated the negative behavior towards the prisoners, the rest of the prison guards went along with it and even actively participated in it.

Many of those individuals may protest their innocence, but their inaction showed acceptance of the deviant behavior coming from someone in a position of authority.

There is one psychologist who played a pivotal role in launching the idea of social psychology and experimentation. His name was John Broadus Watson. He was a proponent of using direct observation of behaviors to help understand their stimuli. He engaged in many experiments that utilized rats in order to make conjectures about how humans would respond in similar circumstances.

Watson realized that connecting a stimulus to a response meant that you could predict how a subject would respond. This meant whoever controlled the stimulus essentially controlled the subject. The subject's response would be a direct result of that stimulus and not of the subject's individual choice. This simple connection between cause and effect is what makes dark psychology so successful and so potentially insidious. If someone already knows what to do to force you into a particular decision, you have been robbed of free will without ever noticing it was gone.

The scientific application of social psychology was not Watson's only interest. When he was ousted from the academic world, he applied his knowledge to the government and private sector, specifically the military and advertising. With the military, he helped design some of the first aptitude tests to evaluate which soldiers would be best for serving in particular positions. These types of tests are still in use today. With advertising, he helped pioneer sales tactics that are also still in use today. It all started with the foundational element of social experiments: observation. He masqueraded as a salesperson in order to observe the average consumer and to reach conclusions on what would motivate them to buy. This led to him recognizing the importance of having a target demographic. A product with a target demographic will be able to customize its slogans to suit the tastes of that part of the population. For example, a new mother will be motivated to buy products that mention safety. He also discovered the immense power of celebrity endorsement. People are psychologically motivated by public figures they admire, so attaching that power to a product promotes sales.

The bottom line of all of his experiments and creations can be summed up in the term dark psychology. If you know how a person will react, that means that you hold their behavior in your hand. With a simple stimulus, you can generate nearly any response you desire. With the power of authority, the power of the stimulus is also increased. Although human beings like to flatter themselves that they are capable of behaving as free-thinking individuals at all times, dark psychology, and these historical experiments, prove otherwise. Humanity has within it the ability to be manipulated and coerced even into torturing another unknown human being. This means that we must learn to be wary of how dark psychology may be shaping our own behavior and also how we can use dark psychology to avoid victimization by the many perpetrators in our midst.

CHAPTER 2
Characteristics Of Dark Psychology

Now that you have begun to grasp the basic concept of dark psychology, here is a deeper dive into its key characteristics. This is not an exhaustive list because a future chapter will take a closer look at these characteristics. Consider this an overview of some of the details of dark psychology. This is another good chapter to revisit, especially when you are looking to gauge whether someone is guilty of using dark psychology against you. It is also another chapter worth revisiting when you want to understand if you are diving too deeply into dark psychology. There is a fine line between dark psychology that has good intentions and dark psychology that is approaching evil. This is a chapter that can help you decipher and evaluate your own emotions before engaging in unnecessarily risky or morally repugnant behaviors.

The Dark Triad

The Dark Triad is a common term used in dark psychology. Although the next chapter will deal with some key terms in dark psychology, it is necessary to have a beginning understanding of this term to truly understand the key points that make someone likely to use dark psychology. The Dark Triad is a hotly contested subject within dark psychology since the term was created only within this century. This means that there is likely much more research to be completed in order to truly understand what each of these terms means and how they manifest themselves in those who practice dark psychology. If you are looking to understand this concept from a different perspective, you may also consider looking into the light triad. It is intended to show the alternative sides of each part of the dark triad. Be sure to look at the explanation of the light triad in the following chapter to learn more.

The term **Dark Triad** is used to describe a trio of personality types that are known to engage in behaviors related to dark psychology. There have been some suggestions for a fourth, but these three are the most commonly discussed. These personality types have components that can overlap. Someone who uses dark psychology may fit into one of these categories. They may fit into a combination of two of these personality types. They may also fit into all three, which means they would be among the most deviant and dangerous individuals you could encounter. Whatever the case may be, if you become aware of someone who fits into one of these categories, you would do well to be on your guard when around them. Regardless of which category they fall into, they can pose a danger to you either emotionally or physically. Use this information to gain a deeper understanding of how they may act and why.

The first personality type of the Dark Triad is a narcissist. Many people are familiar with the term narcissism, but not many people are as familiar with a true narcissistic personality. A true narcissist goes beyond someone who is simply self-interested. True narcissism is so pervasive within these individuals that they cannot act outside of its constraints. They are made to be a narcissist and cannot see another way.

A **narcissist** believes with every fiber of their being that they are the most important person on earth. They are so completely drawn into this feeling that they are often blind to the needs and wants of others. They will always and in any situation center their needs over those of others, regardless of the consequences. This does not come from a choice, necessarily, but is it the product of their belief system. Their belief system has dictated that they are the center of everything, and it would not only be ill-advised but nearly impossible to convince a narcissist that their belief is wrong.

True narcissists often have intense and overpowering personalities in social settings. They tend to self-aggrandize and exaggerate in such a way that benefits themselves and no one else. If they are telling a story, they will be the hero of that story every time. This is not just self-delusion. They truly believe that they are the best of the best, that no one can beat them in any way. Although many will see that this is an act, those susceptible to and unaware of dark psychology tactics may easily become the victim of a narcissist. From a certain perspective, a narcissist may be a very charismatic and appealing figure. After all, their lies will paint them as the epitome of humanity, someone who is not only desirable but enviable. This can have a magnetic draw for those who may wish they were as confident and self-assured as the narcissist.

A final trait of narcissists is the unending need for attention. They will always place themselves at the center of any event and feel an overpowering need to be the focus of all the attention. Their ultimate desire is to be centerstage while everyone watches them in awe, and they will constantly seek to have an audience to watch them as they perform. Of course, their performances will feature them as the dominant figure and will often include others only if they increase the desirability of the narcissist or make them a more enviable figure.

When you combine all of these traits, a narcissist can be a nefarious individual if someone is naively drawn into their performance and actually believes what they say. Since most narcissists are pathological liars and exaggerators, a victim could find themselves falling for a person who quite literally does not exist. However, the narcissist can be such a convincing performer that the victim will be in denial for a long time and may even be the narcissist's top defender. If the victim has no reason to doubt the narcissist, they will, of course, support them. The narcissist is first and foremost an exceptional liar and performer, and many who perhaps suffer low self-esteem will be blindly drawn into this fantasy person. After all, who wouldn't want to be the narcissist? If only their lies were true.

The second personality type is related to the first but is lacking in showmanship. This is called Machiavellianism. While narcissists use lies to uplift themselves, a Machiavellian will use lies for personal gain. This eliminates the performative nature of the lies and can make them harder to detect.

Machiavellianism is the use of strategic deception and manipulation. This means a Machiavellian will use their words not to build themselves up but to trick you into becoming their performer. They will convince you to perform whatever they think will benefit them. They do not care how they achieve this result, only that they achieve it. They are goal-oriented at all times, which can make them vicious when they fully engage their powers.

Strategic deception is essentially lying with a purpose and lying in such a way that the listener will not know they are being lied to. Machiavellians are expert liars who will talk you in circles until you are so utterly lost in their lies that you cannot see where the lie began. Unlike narcissists, Machiavellians' lies are not about boosting their self-image. They have lied with clear intent and with a clear design for what they want to achieve. Strategic planning is the guiding principle behind their lies, so they will have formulated a clear plan before inflicting these lies on their victim. They will not jeopardize their goal with a poor lie but will use careful preparation to lure their victim.

Strategic manipulation is another trait of a Machiavellian. Strategic manipulation means they not only use their words to create believable lies, but also that they use those lies to manipulate you into certain behaviors. Their lies do not stop at believability. Instead, their lies are the catalysts for the behaviors they want you to perform. The Machiavellian has a deep understanding of the cause and effect relationship discussed in the first chapter. This is what makes them such masterful manipulators. They know in advance and after careful study exactly what to do and say to make their lies believable and to make them actionable. You will become their puppet as they pull the invisible strings to get you to do anything, while you remain blissfully unaware.

Machiavellians can be even harder to detect than narcissists because their motives may not be as clear. While it is easier to spot a narcissist because they direct everything to themselves, Machiavellians are much more subtle. They are not in the business of centering themselves but instead lie to achieve any number of motives. Unless you have a deep insight into their motivations, you may not be able to detect a Machiavellian at work. Their design may only become evident after it is too late. That is how intensely talented they are at deception and manipulation. You could be in their power before you would even know what happened. You could also be in a position where you could not fight the consequences of what the Machiavellian set in motion. After all, although the Machiavellian manipulated you, you still engaged in the action. You could argue that you did not do it freely or understand the consequences, but, depending on the situation, it can be impossible to fight back once a Machiavellian has reached their goal. They can always argue that you had a choice, and you chose to do as they desired.

The final personality type in the Dark Triad is psychopaths. Unlike narcissists and Machiavellians, psychopaths do not always have a clear design in mind or a clear focus to motivate their behaviors. This makes them highly unpredictable and nefarious. It has also made them the subject of massive amounts of study, speculation, and intrigue. You could even call them fascinating, although it would be a morbid fascination. It is difficult for someone who lies outside the realm of psychopathy to fully understand how and why they behave as they do. It is reminiscent of the phrase it's like a train wreck you see coming: you can't look away, even if it would be wiser to do so.

Psychopaths are characterized by their impulsive behavior and the absence of empathy. However, within the Dark Triad, psychopath refers merely to a personality type, not to a clinical diagnosis of psychopathy. In other words, a psychopathic personality may display some psychopathic traits but not to the extent that a clinical psychologist would diagnose them as a psychopath. For the sake of this text, they will be referred to as psychopaths, but understand that there is a difference between someone who is diagnosed versus someone who shows traits.

A psychopath's impulsivity makes them highly unpredictable and drastically different from a Machiavellian or a narcissist. The narcissists focus their decisions on themselves. The Machiavellians focus on manipulating those around them. Psychopaths may not have any clear motivation besides the fact that they enjoy witnessing chaos or pain. Their actions do not stem from careful study or strategy. If they want something, they go for it instantaneously, without prior warning. This can be both beneficial and detrimental to the psychopath. The complete lack of planning can mean it's much easier for the psychopath to move undetected. You cannot connect their behavior to any motives, other than they wanted to do it. However, impulsivity also equates to higher risk. It is possible that the lack of planning means they are sloppy. This sloppiness could mean them risking detection more often. Either way, impulsivity is dangerous in someone who engages in dark psychology. Predictability means safety. Psychopaths defy that safety.

The most sinister quality of a psychopath is the absence of empathy. They do not and cannot place themselves in someone else's perspective. They are blithely unaware of how their actions may affect the feelings of others and do not have an understanding of many human emotions. This means that they are more likely to behave in violent ways. Violence does not phase them because someone else's pain causes no sympathetic reaction in their own feelings. They could hear someone's screams and tears and be completely unmoved. They may even enjoy it because they do not understand normal human emotional reactions. They have no concept of what it means to cause someone else pain. What is even worse, they do not care. They cannot grasp what it means to care.

The combination of impulsivity and a lack of empathy makes psychopaths perhaps the most sinister of the three personality types. They move through life as they see fit, when they see fit, with complete disregard for the feelings of others. Feelings quite literally do not matter to them, which makes them most likely to become violent or to engage in risky criminal behavior. They do not see how these behaviors are objectionable because they do not see outside their own impulsive desires.

Psychopaths are most closely related to Machiavellians because of their tendency to manipulate to suit themselves, while narcissists are completely self-centered. However, there is a possibility that all of these personality types may be found in one person for a combination of two.

A narcissist with Machiavellian tendencies will be characterized by self-importance but also by manipulative behaviors. Rather than limit their lies to those that build their self-image, they will both exaggerate to elevate themselves and to manipulate those around them into behaving in certain ways. These two personality types working in conjunction characterize many of those who hold positions of power. Individuals are drawn to the appeal of the narcissist and are kept in control by the manipulation of the Machiavellian. Some may even describe this combination as charming because the person clearly works to benefit themselves but will stroke your own ego enough to coerce you into behaving in all sorts of ways. They are self-centered, but their lies can make you believe that they are thinking only of you. This is a tempting combination for those who may be psychologically vulnerable.

A narcissist with psychopathic tendencies will still be self-important but will also engage in risk-taking behavior that ignores the needs of others. This personality combination is less likely to be appealing to others because a narcissistic psychopath will not be able to clearly understand others' feelings. However, they will still be a pathological liar. This kind of individual will often come across as callous and unfeeling. That does not mean they cannot be dangerous to others. There are those who will fall prey to the charisma of the narcissistic side of their personality and become complicit in their psychopathic behaviors because they trust the narcissist. If someone were to believe their persona, they could be easily tempted into justifying the person's illicit behaviors.

A Machiavellian with psychopathic tendencies is perhaps one of the most dangerous personality combinations. Although psychopaths do not understand emotion, the calculating manipulation of a Machiavellian may help them learn to mimic these emotions. They will mimic emotions in order to create a desired response. This, combined with extreme impulsivity, means that Machiavellian psychopaths are very difficult to detect. Think of them as chameleons. They understand that they are not emotionally made like other people, and so they learn to put on whatever emotional response necessary to elicit a desirable behavior in their victim. It is a disconcerting conglomeration of personality traits. They may not be as appealing as a narcissist, but they will still be able to use performative manipulation that is convincing and motivating for the victim.

It is possible to have an individual who shows traits characteristic of all three personality types. This type of individual would be towards the darkest end of the dark psychology spectrum. First, they would be an exceptional performer who is utterly convinced of their own superiority. Second, they will use their performances to draw in and manipulate everyone around them. Their motives will be entirely selfish, and their means will be without limitations. Finally, they will engage all of these powerful traits to create chaos whenever and however they desire, all while completely ignoring the impact of their decisions and manipulations. In short, they live solely to control others to make themselves feel good. Their lack of empathy also means they do not fall prey to their own feelings or the feelings of others. They are emotionally flat and will only use emotion as a manipulation tactic or as a way to gain even more attention. If you become a victim of someone who falls into this category, you will have an incredibly difficult time seeing and understanding how you became the prey of such a predator. It could take months or even years of reflection to fully understand the ways in which they have controlled your life decisions and your emotional responses. That being said, it is not your fault if you find yourself a victim of one are all of these personalities. They are the product of the darker side of humanity, and the best you can do is to educate yourself further, so you do not become a victim again in the future. It is as much human to have characteristics of dark psychology as it is to be a victim of dark psychology.

Other Characteristics

Although many practitioners of dark psychology will have strong connections to a personality type in the Dark Triad, that is not always the case. There are a number of traits that are somewhat similar to these three, but they are still noteworthy in your study of dark psychology.

A related but less prevalent form of narcissism is egoism. **Egoism** is also self-centered but is more about the benefits the individual enjoys. They want things to go their way and have no concern about possible effects. They want to bask in the glory of something that makes them happy, and that is the only bottom line.

Another dark psychology trait is moral disengagement. This would be most directly connected to psychopathy. **Moral disengagement** means the individual can compartmentalize their feelings and set aside their personal morals when making a decision or taking action. While a psychopath has no choice in whether they can understand feelings, someone who uses moral disengagement plans to set aside their morals in order to act like a psychopath might act. In other words, they can choose to ignore their feelings of guilt and empathy. They can then reengage their morals after committing whatever act went against those morals and behave and react morally in other situations. This is a tricky character trait because it means someone could be perceived as more humane than a psychopath, yet they are almost worse because they have an innate understanding of empathy. They simply choose to set it aside.

The next trait is psychological entitlement. This would be most closely related to narcissism. **Psychological entitlement** is the deep belief that the individual is deserving of something above all others. They are like a narcissist because they are immersed in the belief that they are the best or the most deserving person. Unlike a narcissist, however, they are not about performance but are about benefits. They feel they deserve whatever is best because their merits surpass all others. This is a firmly held belief and not something the individual may be conscious of.

Spitefulness is another potential trait within dark psychology. It can be connected to both Machiavellianism and psychopathy. **Spitefulness** can be summed up by the word revenge. This type of individual is motivated by a need to retaliate. This can manifest as violent behaviors. What makes this trait so dangerous is that it is so all-consuming that the individual will do whatever it takes to achieve their revenge, even if they harm themselves in the process. This makes them somewhat Machiavellian because they are centered on a clear goal, but it also makes them psychopathic because they engage in any behavior regardless of consequences to others or themselves. It is an unfeeling trait.

Self-interest can also characterize dark psychology. It is connected to narcissism and Machiavellianism. **Self-interest** is what it sounds like: a desire to benefit oneself. It most often includes behaviors that will enhance a person's wealth or social status. It is similar to narcissism because it is entirely focused on the individual. It is like Machiavellianism in that it has a clear goal. Individuals who display this characteristic are more easily detected because of the clear motivations for the person's behaviors.

One of the most disturbing characteristics of dark psychology is sadism. It is most closely connected to psychopathy. **Sadism** is the desire to cause harm because of the satisfaction that it brings. This harm can be physical or emotional. What is most concerning about this trait is that the perpetrator truly achieves pleasure or enjoyment from witnessing the harm inflicted on the victim. This connects to psychopathy because it shows a lack of innate empathy. The victim's feelings are only of consequence because they bring satisfaction to the perpetrator.

Use these characteristics to understand how dark psychology may be at work in your own life, and use it to understand how to analyze and break free. Once you truly understand, dark psychology will no longer be a source of fear but a source of freedom.

CHAPTER 3
Dark Psychology Terms Explained

This chapter is meant to serve as a reference guide for you not only as you read this text but also as you need to return to it to refresh yourself on some of the key terms in the field. You will notice that there is some overlap between terms in this chapter and terms explained in other chapters. That is to enable you to have one location to return to if you only need a quick reminder rather than a full reread of an entire chapter. Please consider this chapter as one of the best tools in this text because it summarizes more succinctly the terms you will need to navigate dark psychology knowledgeably. It is also a perfect way to introduce a friend to some of the concepts you are studying. Let them take a peek and see if this text could become their guide as well.

Basic Dark Psychology Terms

Arsonist: An arsonist is an individual who expresses not just a fascination with but an obsession with setting fires. An arsonist can be related to dark psychology because they are engaging in a behavior, which most often is done for their benefit, sometimes even pleasure, and is done at great cost to others. There is a predator, and there is a victim. What is less present in an arsonist is the components of manipulation and control. It could be said that an arsonist is seeking to manipulate and control the authorities and takes pride in the fact that they can get away with it. An arsonist's relationship to dark psychology would need to be analyzed on a case-by-case basis.

Brainwashing: Brainwashing is the systematic and methodical process of a victim fully believing in the power of the predator. The victim may not even acknowledge to themselves or others that they are being controlled. They will be wrapped up in the delusion that they are safer with the predator and must stay with the predator at all costs. It is characterized by many dark psychology practices, such as fatigue inducement, starvation, social-isolation, and more. It is also commonly used in organizations of people, such as cults. Its results can be notoriously difficult to reverse. Victims may spend decades continuing to believe that the perpetrator is still trustworthy.

Choice restriction: Choice restriction is an act in which the predator provides the victim with a series of choices but omits the choice they do not want the victim to make. In this way, the victim feels as though they are controlling their choices, but the reality is the choice that is undesirable for the predator is completely absent. It creates a delusional sense of power for the victim and makes it much harder to see the predator's manipulation. The victim will defend themselves by arguing that they always had a choice when the truth is they only had the choices the predator allowed.

Dark Continuum: The Dark Continuum is a spectrum of behavior that can be connected to dark psychology. This continuum encompasses all kinds of deviant and predatory behavior. It has a range that can go from purposeful, planned actions to wanton chaos. It can also go from mere thoughts of victimization to impulsive, violent, criminal acts. A person can travel along this spectrum at different points in their life according to how deeply they dive into dark psychology and how actively they work to use it on a daily basis. It is most likely that the majority of people will stay relatively low on the spectrum and not progress to its most devious end.

Dark Factor: Dark Factor is the amount of potential someone has to not only possess traits related to dark psychology but to put those traits into action on a regular basis. Someone's Dark Factor could be increased by life experiences, such as trauma during formative years or an unstable and unhealthy upbringing. These, combined with perhaps a personality type within the Dark Triad, will increase the amount of Dark Factor a person is likely to have. It is easy to say that someone has a large amount of Dark Factor because of circumstances out of their control, but that does not guarantee they will act on them. Be careful to avoid assumptions based on these indicators.

Dark psychology: This term encompasses the concept that every human has within them the innate ability to victimize another for no clear evolutionary purpose. The most easily identifiable characteristic of dark psychology is a desire to manipulate and control others for a variety of motivations, including physical, emotional, and psychological desires. Some would sum it up as mind control. However, it is a powerful human characteristic, which everyone is born with, but not all choose to engage. Everyone is capable, but not all act upon the impulses and motivations associated with dark psychology. Please refer to Chapter 1 for a much more comprehensive look into what makes dark psychology such a unique and fascinating subject area.

Dark sense of humor psychology: This area of psychology suggests that those who enjoy a darker sense of humor have higher levels of intelligence. These levels are higher both cognitively and verbally. It shows an ability to analyze and find the wit within "gallows humor." Those who enjoy dark humor also tend to have an ability to practice more readily and to strike the difficult balance of intellectual enjoyment and dark content. It is not necessarily a major component of dark psychology, but it is a related field and could still be another indicator that someone is more likely to practice tactics of dark psychology.

Dark Singularity: Dark Singularity is the deepest, darkest, most abhorrent portion of the Dark Continuum. Dark Singularity could be thought of as evil. However, it is not simply evil, but what you may call the pinnacle of evil, incomprehensible, and completely outside of the boundaries of normal, predictable, justifiable, rational, and moral human behavior. This area of dark psychology is one few will ever approach, and those who do will be regarded as almost subhuman because of their ability to behave in such unfathomable ways. It is not likely that anyone would ever reach the point of Dark Singularity because it would make the perpetrator almost inhuman in the eyes of others.

Dark Triad: This is a term for the three personality types most often associated with the use of dark psychology. Those three personality types are narcissists, Machiavellians, and psychopaths. There is some debate that there is a fourth personality type, the everyday sadist, but the scholarship most frequently focuses on the three personality types listed above. Please note that the term psychopath in this text does not refer to a psychological diagnosis of psychopathy by a medical professional but instead refers to characteristics exhibited as an aspect of someone's personality. For more details about the three personality types of the Dark Triad, read the definitions in this list or return to Chapter Two for an in-depth look at each of them and related personality characteristics.

Darkness Manipulation: This term is used to describe the power someone possesses if they are a practitioner of dark psychology. This power can be cultivated if someone chooses to actively pursue and study dark psychology to become a master manipulator and mind controller. However, there is a suggestion from other theories, like the Dark Triad, that certain personality types are more likely to already have the skill of darkness manipulation. It is possibly the result of their dark psychology being closer to the surface of their consciousness than that of most other people.

Egoism: This is an obsessive personality trait in which an individual is concerned only with what will benefit them. They are so preoccupied with this goal that they will completely ignore how it may impact those around them. The person's sense of self-importance is so strong that they cannot comprehend why they would need to think about how pursuing their own success may negatively affect others.

Fatigue inducement: Fatigue inducement is sleep-deprivation or fatigue-producing acts. Once fatigue is induced, the victim will be so deep into their fatigue that they will begin to change what they are saying and doing so that it will make the perpetrator happy, even if that means lying. This is a common practice within law enforcement and military tactics. The victim is much more willing to be compliant when they have been systematically deprived of rest. This is frequently combined with starvation to create an even stronger effect.

Gift giving: Gift giving is what it sounds like, but it is more specific than just giving a present to someone. Gift giving is providing a present or desirable item to someone so that the other person will feel the need to reciprocate. It essentially guilts them into returning the favor in some way, whatever that may be. In other words, this scenario means there are always strings attached to the gift, and the receiver will be reminded about the gift as a way to control and manipulate them into doing something or giving something in return.

Guilt inducement: Guilt inducement is the act of making a victim feel guilty by expressing some kind of sadness, or other negative feeling, that can only be alleviated by the victim. This usually comes in the form of a passive-aggressive comment or a comment that is meant to sound caring or thoughtful but instead makes the victim feel they have done something wrong and must do whatever it takes to fix the perceived problem. The victim is under the delusion that they have become the source of the perpetrator's angst and must make amends in whatever way the perpetrator may want.

Internet predator: An internet predator may not seem at first to be always closely linked with dark psychology, but when you stop to think about it, the goal of those who engage in cyberbullying, cyberstalking, and other web crimes are predators seeking a victim. That is the core of dark psychology, so dark psychology internet threats are as relevant as face-to-face threats. They still carry with them an intent to create harm that has no evolutionary purpose. The only shared goal in every dark psychology tactic is to control or manipulate. That is also the goal of internet predators. These connections are explored more fully in Chapter 6.

Light Triad: The Light Triad is meant to be the direct opposite of the Dark Triad. In this triad, the characteristics are all about performing acts that benefit others rather than victimize others. The three components of the Light Triad are Kantianism, faith in humanity, and humanism. This would be an excellent source of research for those who are studying this text as a way to understand what not to do when interacting with others and how to avoid being associated with negative motives and predatory behavior.

Love denial: Love denial is the conscious and purposeful withholding of "love." This can come in the form of refusing to outwardly show affection. It can also come in the form of ignoring the victim until the predator gets what they want. It is meant to push the victim into doing as the predator wants so that the predator will once again "love" the victim and show attention and affection. The use of the word "love" is quite misleading because this act is the antithesis of true love. The perpetrator only does enough to keep the victim as their prey. They are not interested in truly loving the victim.

Love flooding: Love flooding is almost self-explanatory because the name says it all. It is the conscious act of completely overwhelming someone with "love." This can come in the form of compliments or affection and is almost always followed by requests for something from the victim. It lures the victim into believing that the predator loves them and that the victim must do what they are being asked to prove they return the love. This goes beyond the common practice of a child saying to a parent, "Mommy/Daddy, I love you so much," and then asking for a toy or candy. Love flooding is much more conscious, less obvious, and the requests are not as benign in nature.

Machiavellian: A Machiavellian is someone who uses lies to manipulate others to help them achieve a self-serving goal. What sets apart Machiavellians is their unparalleled ability to verbally and emotionally control others. Their lies are often the product of careful study and preparation so that the victim is completely unaware that they are being coerced into a series of actions already pre-planned by the Machiavellian. They are ruthless and driven only by the need to benefit themselves. What makes them so sinister is the precision with which they craft their lies. It makes them difficult to perceive, even if you're looking for their traits.

Mind games: Mind games are not only for the movies. They are actual strategic decisions made to coerce a victim into a sense of powerlessness and to make the perpetrator appear infinitely superior. It is the use of a number of psychological strategies all at once that methodically direct the thoughts, emotions, and actions of the intended victim. Those who use mind games are not only practitioners of dark psychology, at least not laymen. These sorts of tactics may be employed in any number of professions as a way to monitor certain individuals, such as criminals, suspected criminals, captives, or even employees. This is a difficult tactic to master but is also dangerous because it can be so complicated and nuanced.

Moral disengagement: When someone is morally disengaged, they have made a conscious choice to "turn off" their moral value in order to commit an immoral act without guilt. They are able to compartmentalize their own conscience in such a way that they will be capable of feeling guilt one moment and completely remorseless the next. This allows them to set aside their humanity when perpetrating some type of victimization or criminal, violent, or deviant act.

Narcissist: A narcissist is someone who is completely self-centered and will use lies to manipulate others into believing their grandiose self-concept. They frequently lie to make themselves appear more important. They constantly crave attention. For this reason, they will enjoy being on stage for a large audience. Whatever action they take, it is to serve one purpose, and that is to increase their perceived importance.

Necrophilia: Necrophilia is the desire to engage in sexual behavior with a corpse. This may sound difficult to connect to dark psychology because the victim is no longer living. However, there can be a deep-seated connection between dark psychology and necrophilia for a fair number of reasons. First and foremost, necrophilia has been connected to difficulties with achieving intimacy and a need to be in control of the intimate act of intercourse. The necrophile has a much higher sense of control when their victim is a corpse. Second, although not true of all cases, it is possible that dark psychology is what was used to entice the victim into the necrophile's path. The necrophile could be the one who killed the victim, which is a brutal exercise of control over another person. This all points clearly back to dark psychology.

Priming: Priming is a type of manipulation that subconsciously affects your decision-making. Priming can be something as straightforward as a verbal signal to something as subtle as product placement in a TV series. It can often be hard to detect unless you are hyper aware of word choice and its effects on your reactions. For example, I might say, "The location was sweltering, like an instant bath in your own sweat, streams pouring down your blistering skin." Within the next minute or two, you may unconsciously begin to feel hot or uncomfortable, perhaps shifting your weight around like you are trying to air out. It could be perfectly pleasant where you are sitting, but the verbal suggestion could be enough to move you to behave in a certain way.

Psychological entitlement: This is a person's belief that their self-worth is so high, they are more deserving than others. They do not simply want what is being asked for but truly believe it should naturally be given to them because of their inherent merit. This means they will not be able to understand when they are denied something, no matter how convincing the counter argument may be.

Psychopath: A psychopath is someone who acts on impulse and has an absence of empathy. They are often considered highly chaotic because it is unclear when and why they will engage in all manner of manipulative, controlling, and even violent behaviors. What characterizes them to the most is an inability to understand and perceive the emotions of others and how their own actions affect others. They may even enjoy witnessing pain or fear because they cannot understand its negative effect on the victim. They are different from a sociopath because they do not have a merely limited conscience but no conscience at all.

Reverse psychology: Reverse psychology has become a common term that most people are familiar with. It is the act of telling someone to do something when, in fact, you want them to do the opposite. This is often effective when the victim is upset with the predator. The predator will say what they want the victim to do, and because the victim is upset and does not want to make the predator happy, they do the opposite. But the predator wanted them to do the opposite all along. These scenarios seem obvious when practiced with small children or in a movie, but reverse psychology is still a common and possibly dangerous tactic within dark psychology.

Sadism: Sadism is a desire to inflict pain because of the enjoyment and perhaps pleasure that it brings. A sadist will engage in any number of violent behaviors in order to enjoy some kind of satisfaction from the pain produced. To them, pain and pleasure are synonymous. This could be their own pain or the pain of others.

Self-interest: This is similar to the idea of being self-centered but is differentiated by the desire to enjoy material and measurable success for oneself. This often comes in the form of an increased social status or increased financial status. It means that a self-interested person will be motivated by what helps them succeed and will be disinterested in how it may help or harm others.

Semantic manipulation: This means the act of using words or phrases with multiple meanings. These word choices allow a predator to deny that they intended a certain interpretation of what they said. This can make the victim feel that they were wrong for thinking the predator meant to hurt them or manipulate them and instead will feel that they were the one who was wrong all along.

Serial killer: A serial killer is defined as a killer who commits three or more murders that occur over a length of a month or longer. There is often a gap of time between the murders, which is what differentiates a serial killer from a mass murderer. Serial killers have a deep connection to dark psychology because they often exhibit one, two, or all three personality types within the Dark Triad. Additionally, serial murders often engage in behaviors that manipulate and control their victims, whether that be through tempting them to go with them willingly or torturing them, so the serial killer feels in control of their fear and pain.

Sociopath: A sociopath is someone who is clinically diagnosed and who is characterized by antisocial behaviors and a limited conscience. They may understand that a certain act is considered morally wrong, but they will move forward with committing the act anyway. This is what sets them apart from a psychopath, someone with no conscience. They are similar in that they both lack the ability to empathize with others.

Spitefulness: Spitefulness is an extreme and consuming need for revenge. Someone who is possessed by spitefulness will have such a powerful urge to retaliate that they will do whatever it takes. They will even risk harm to themselves, as long as it increases the likelihood that they will feel avenged.

Subliminal influence: Subliminal influence is the use of embedded visual and auditory stimuli to get the viewer to act in certain ways. This is actually an integral tactic for magicians. They prime you to choose a certain way or use a certain word by using subliminal influencers. This is a highly strategic practice and one that is most common in fields like advertising.

Withdrawal: Withdrawal is the act of the predator ignoring the victim in some way. This could mean the predator remains near the victim but will give them the silent treatment. This could also mean the predator completely withdraws from the presence of the victim, leaving the victim alone. This act of depriving the victim of the predator is meant to make the victim actively crave the predator's presence and acquiesce to whatever the predator is demanding of the victim.

CHAPTER 4
Typical Tactics Of Dark Psychology

You now understand what dark psychology is, its key characteristics, and its key terms. However, part of what makes dark psychology a source of fascination is its tactics. These strategies are what make the perpetrator the puppeteer and the victim an often-unwitting puppet. The purpose of sharing these tactics is not for you to utilize them so much as it is for you to recognize them and avoid them. To that end, each tactic will be explained and then followed by a few ideas on how to detect that tactic and address so you will not be the victim for long, if at all.

Strategies in Detail

The first strategy we will explore is one of the most basic, and that is deception. Or, more simply put, lying. It seems simple enough at first. You "stretch" or "bend" the truth to make something easier for yourself, and the victim is most likely completely unaware and unharmed. This could be something rather benign, like telling a friend you're running late because of traffic, when in fact you overslept. It's something nearly everyone has done. It is a "small" lie that still benefits the liar. However, within dark psychology, deception is an art form. It is the basis of so many of the atrocities perpetrators commit.

Lying within dark psychology can come in two forms. One would be lying because of careful study and planning. The other is the result of total impulse. Both can be incredibly damaging for a victim, and both have their pros and cons. Planning, of course, has the added benefit that the perpetrator can think through any number of scenarios that may expose their lie. In this way, they can prepare for eventualities and have perhaps another lie ready to back up the first if necessary. The detriment to this kind of lying is that strategic liars almost always have to layer their lies to continue to make them believable over extended periods of time. This means keeping track of who was lied to and what lies they were told. A quick slip could mean the whole set of lies comes tumbling down and exposes the perpetrator. There is also a possibility that the perpetrator will spend so long planning the lie that one of the factors involved will change and ruin the plan, sending the perpetrator back to stage one of their planning. Those perpetrators who lie more impulsively are often good at improvising. They can lie quickly and make it believable, and they can craft it instantaneously. This avoids the tedium of planning and can give the lie less of a "studied" air. This type of lying could also be much easier for someone who plans to do something to the victim shortly after lying that will distract them from the lie. This kind of lying is dangerous because there is a chance that the victim will discover the lie as quickly as it was told. After all, the liar did not take any disruptions or other eventualities into account. Regardless of which kind of lie someone may choose, lying is a cornerstone of dark psychology.

Most of the tips for avoiding a liar or spotting a lie may seem obvious, but it is important to remember that someone well-versed in dark psychology will be lying on a different level than you are used to. The easiest way to investigate whether you are being lied to is to seek concrete evidence of the lie. This may sound devious in itself, but that is only true if you are investigating without just cause. Concrete evidence means something verifiable and tangible, such as a written document or a security video. Be wary of eye-witness accounts. It is entirely possible that you are talking to someone who is also part of the lie or to another victim who will corroborate the lie because they are in the perpetrator's power. An even more simple tactic is to directly confront the individual about the situation and demand they provide the concrete evidence themselves. After all, if they have nothing to hide, there should be no reason that they would withhold that evidence.

The second strategy is cheating. You may be saying to yourself that this one is too obvious. However, a good cheater can make it far fast if they are methodical and careful. Cheating is not just looking at a neighbor's paper during a test. Cheating can also be cheating within a relationship. This kind of cheating is also closely connected to the first strategy, lying. You cannot achieve a successful cheat without the ability to lie. This then ties into a third strategy, denial. A liar who has decided to cheat may indeed get caught. After the perpetrator is caught, their instinct will be to deny the charges. This is not only natural but intentional for someone who uses dark psychology regularly. They may not have expected it, but they will formulate a denial quickly. The denial deflects from the lie and causes you, the victim, to defend yourself instead of the perpetrator defending themselves.

Cheating and denial are closely related, so we will talk about avoidance tactics for both at the same time. A clear sign of cheating is when something appears to come too easily for the perpetrator and is not in line with their normal behavior and/or achievement levels. If it seems abnormal, it more than likely is. Do not be afraid to trust your gut, and again, look for the concrete evidence. To avoid the problems of denial, stick to facts. Present what you know in clear terms that leave no room for denial. After each fact, demand that the perpetrator verifies what you have said so that they cannot try to backtrack later. If they continue to try to deny, then follow your facts with requests for concrete evidence. There is no room for denial when you are asking them to show their innocence. Again, if they are truly innocent, there will be no need to hide anything that proves it.

A perhaps unsuspected dark psychology tactic is apologizing. This is a powerful tool because it is something that has always been presented as positive. After all, we all learned in school that when you cause harm or make a mistake, you must apologize before healing can begin, and then everyone can move forward. A perpetrator is aware of this process and will use apologies to get to you to move on quickly from what went wrong. The danger in this is that you will too easily forget how many times they have committed the offense or may miss a pattern of behavior that would lead you to discover their lies sooner. Apologies also make a victim feel better and more at ease. It seems unlikely that someone who is "evil" would be willing to apologize. We frequently equate apologies to goodness. Just because they said "sorry" does not mean it is true or that they will not engage in the manipulative behavior again.

To avoid the danger of apologies, try to give yourself reflection time after the fact. At that moment, you will be caught up in your emotions, emotions the perpetrator may have stirred up on purpose. After the conversation is over, think through what began the issue. Ask yourself if it was something that could truly be fixed by an apology. Ask yourself if it's something they've done before. Ask yourself if you can think of other times they've used an apology to avoid an uncomfortable situation. Were any of those issues truly resolved? Or did the negative behavior resurface anyway? A good way to make sure an apology is not devoid of merit is to demand that concrete and measurable actions be connected to the apology. If they are sorry, they should also demonstrate altered behavior or present a plan for how they will improve in the future.

Another tactic that may quickly follow an apology is doing favors for you. This may sound kind or even thoughtful, and for a normal person, it may be. But for someone who is using dark psychology to victimize you, the favors serve one purpose, distraction. You will be so caught up in the emotional euphoria that comes from having something done for you that you will neglect to properly assess whether the predator fixed the problem they caused in the first place.

A quick way to spot genuine favors is if the person mentions why they are doing the favor. They may say something like, "I am doing this to show you..." and fill in that blank with whatever issues it is they need to work on. You will know it's meant to be a distraction if it has no discernible connection to what went wrong. It seems to be completely random and unmotivated. This may sound like a positive experience, unexpected kindness, but you must ask yourself if it was something the perpetrator could have easily done on impulse or something that required planning. Ask yourself if it looks like a random act but obviously took some planning. Then ask yourself if it happened right after a problem arose. If that is the case, then they may be trying to make you believe in them again without wanting you to make the connection between the favor and the victimizing act.

Another manipulative strategy is showing sympathy. Again, this may sound ridiculous because showing sympathy is supposed to be a good thing. Showing sympathy is an important way to show that you care about someone else's feelings. You are correct in most cases, but in the case of dark psychology, you may need to think again. The sympathy is only necessary because of what the perpetrator did. They are trying to comfort you when you would not be suffering if they had not victimized you first. As with favors, sympathy is meant to be a distraction from what created the need for sympathy. You will be feeling comforted and cared for, which is a pleasant experience. However, once you take a step back, you will be able to remind yourself that you only need comfort because the perpetrator caused you pain.

If you want to stop negative sympathy, the easiest step is to separate yourself from the perpetrator. You will not be able to reflect and think clearly when the perpetrator can still easily manipulate you with another round of lies, denials, apologies, favors, and more sympathy. They have an arsenal of tactics now to get you to move on from noticing the heart of what they did and why they did it. Another good idea is to present the scenario to someone else you find trustworthy. See what their initial reaction is. As the victim, you may be too close to the situation to see it clearly. An outside perspective may show you just how ridiculous the perpetrator is and how manipulative their behavior is becoming. Even better, ask yourself if there is someone who has been in your place before. Maybe the perpetrator has another victim you could contact who could validate your experiences and help you see your way out of their lies even faster.

Although seeking out other victims could be helpful when they are accessible, if they are inaccessible, the perpetrator may use them to make you feel inferior. They may start comparing you to the other victim or simply another person. This comparison is meant to manipulate you into going on the defensive. Once you do that, you have taken the focus off of the perpetrator and put it on yourself instead. The person they choose to compare you to is also important to notice. They may strategically choose someone who makes you feel inferior in some way or someone you dislike. Either one will create a powerful emotional reaction within you. Now the person you are thinking of is the one they are comparing you to. You have lost sight of the perpetrator again, which is exactly what they want.

When a perpetrator begins to compare you to someone else, it is best to stop yourself before you respond. Ask the perpetrator to give you some time, which they will not like and may throw them off. Then you can assess why they chose that person for comparison. You can also assess if there is a genuine connection between the person they compared you to and the situation at hand. If there is a connection, then they may genuinely be trying to show you how you may be a part of the problem, too. If there is no connection, then the perpetrator's goal was to make you defend yourself and once again distract you from what they did.

If all their other tactics have failed, a perpetrator may try to turn the whole situation on its head by complaining about you. Once again, the focus will be shifted, and you will be on the defensive. They may even try to make it seem like you are the perpetrator, placing themselves in the role of victim. This will most likely cause you to become angry and will almost always cause you to start defending yourself. Defending yourself means they have control again. They are making you do all of the work while they keep pushing your emotional and psychological buttons, creating whatever reaction they want.

When a perpetrator of dark psychology begins to start complaining about you rather than allowing you to confront them, it is best to make yourself and them go back to the beginning. Ask yourself and them what started this conversation or situation in the first place. What was the catalyst for all this chaos? If the answer is the perpetrator, then you have successfully controlled them rather than allowing them to control you. If they continue to try this tactic and complain about you more, then try to pacify them with a compromise. It will lure them into a false sense of security. You could say that you will happily let them confront you about their complaints but only after you have finished having your say. The important part is that you maintain control of the focus of the situation.

If a perpetrator successfully complains about you and has put you on the defensive, it is likely that they will next attempt to lure you into feelings of guilt and shame. For example, if they denied that they lied and used another lie to prove themselves innocent, they may say to you, "It's easy to see you don't trust me. You can't understand how much that hurts me." So now they have successfully complained that you do not trust them and have preyed on your feelings by making you feel bad that you hurt them. This will make your emotional focus shift from righteous anger to guilt and shame. Now you will feel that you are paranoid and cruel to not trust the perpetrator. Even worse, you will be worrying about their feelings when the true victim in all of this has always been you.

This is one of the more difficult tactics to fight against because we have been so programmed to let guilt and shame overtake our emotions. What you could do is let the situation play out and let the perpetrator feel they won. Then later, after you have overcome those feelings of guilt and shame, you can readily walk yourself back through the conversation and assess if you truly did anything wrong in the situation. If the answer is no, then do not let the perpetrator feel in control for long. Force them back into the conversation and start it with the correct focus, which is what the perpetrator did to victimize you.

If a perpetrator is intent on their goal of victimizing you no matter what, they may resort to emotional blackmail. Emotional blackmail is a form of manipulation that uses emotions to get you to act as the perpetrator desires. Since it relies on manipulation, that means it falls into the category of dark psychology. This process has a few steps before the perpetrator will be successful. They will begin by presenting their demand, what they want you to do. It is likely you will resist, whether directly or indirectly. Resistance is a natural part of the emotional blackmailing process. To fight back, the perpetrator will apply more pressure to their demand, perhaps by telling you to do it out of love or that you owe them (perhaps because of one of the favors they performed) or trying to show you why the demand is a good thing. If the pressure does not create the desired effect, the perpetrator will move onto threats. These threats will be related to some of the key terms explored in Chapter 3, like withdrawal and love denial. As with everything a perpetrator does, these threats will be designed specifically to manipulate you and ensure you will remain their victim. It is most likely at this point that you will give up because the threat is too great. This lets the perpetrator not only know that they were successful but also that this is a strategy they can use successfully on you again.

This is perhaps one of the most difficult tactics from which to break free. After all, the threat that they use is tailored to what will provoke the deepest response from you. That is why dark psychology perpetrators are so dangerous. It is more than likely that you will not be able to avoid the emotional blackmail within the context of the moment, and that does not mean you are a failure. What it means is that you are human and susceptible, as we all are, especially when someone is as adept as the perpetrator at manipulation and coercion. What you have to do is assess, when it is all done, whether you have just done something that you would never have considered doing for another person. Imagine the scenario you were just in with another person in your life. If it seems far-fetched or sounds ridiculous, that is because it is. You were victimized. Once you have seen this, the next step is much harder. That is to use a dark psychology tactic to protect yourself and withdraw. If the perpetrator was able to get what they wanted, they are almost guaranteed to do it again and only increase the level of threat the more you resist. To break the cycle, you have to remove yourself entirely. After all, they knew you well enough to manipulate you into behaving in ways you may never have considered before or even find disgusting after the fact. If they have that kind of power already with just a few sentences, imagine how much worse they could become. If you feel tempted to return, find an accountability buddy who keeps you on track. Ask them what they would do and why before you take any action yourself. Surround yourself with allies who are as disconnected from the perpetrator as possible, so they do not also try to victimize them.

The final tactic we will discuss is avoidance. The perpetrator may have exhausted all of their dark psychology resources, but you may be shocked by how effective avoidance can be. As we learned with the Dark Triad, practitioners of dark psychology can often have huge, charismatic personalities that they have designed to lure people in. That is a magnet for victims that can be difficult to resist. After all, if you have been their victim, then there is some part of yourself you entrusted to them. That creates a bond between you, however sinister it may be. Think of it like you are an addict in recovery who quits cold turkey but knows their substance of choice is nearby but not accessible. That is plain torture. It can be the same for a victim. The perpetrator had an undeniable draw for the victim, and giving up on the perpetrator, at least the idea of who the perpetrator is, is like giving up something that made you feel like you never have before.

You have to treat avoidance the same way an addict would maintain their sobriety, and that is through concrete steps, accountability, and a strong support system. The concrete steps could be a combination of the practices mentioned above to avoid being manipulated. Accountability could come in the form of writing reflections when you feel the urge to reach out to the perpetrator. It could be having someone specific you call when you are tempted to find the perpetrator. The strong support system can often be the most difficult component because there is a strong likelihood that the perpetrator will have isolated you from whatever support system you had before you met them. They will also have deluded you into believing those people would never help you again. As with much of what perpetrators say, that is likely a lie. Reach out to those people and reconstruct that support system. They will be what keeps the perpetrator at bay and ensures you will never be victimized again.

This chapter may have you questioning everything about your relationships with others, but that is not its purpose. Be wary of thinking this level of predator is present everywhere. It's not that they don't exist but that few perpetrators are truly successful in deluding victims for long. Only those who lie further along the Dark Continuum will engage nearly every tactic mentioned above in such a way that they can convince a victim to do whatever they want. There are also many perpetrators within dark psychology who will not use many of these tactics because they are more interested in short-term victims than long-term victims. The point is to be aware but not paranoid. Darkness exists, yes, but it is not the dominant trait in humanity.

CHAPTER 5
Average People Engaging In Dark Psychology

You now have a strong foundation in dark psychology concepts and in the most common personality types and tactics used in dark psychology. You may be thinking that you could stop there, but then you would miss out on a fascinating area of dark psychology. Dark psychology is not only used by master manipulators in grand schemes but is also a common tool used by common people. In fact, you most likely have interacted with one of these people within the past year, month, week, or even day and thought they were average or normal. They are not on the darkest end of the Dark Continuum but rather use dark psychology as a part of their everyday lives to drive others to behave in predictable ways. Some may even argue that these kinds of people should not be thrown in with the term dark psychology, but they would be wrong. Always remember that the only key ingredient for dark psychology is a perpetrator who is looking to victimize. That perpetrator may not be seeking to actively harm the other person. What they are doing may not look "harmful" at all. However, that does not change the fact that their actions are construed to manipulate others, often for personal gain, thereby creating the necessary perpetrator/victim dynamic. Dive into this chapter to understand how dark psychology is at work all around you, even if it may look completely innocuous.

Everyday Manipulators

Dark psychology is most closely associated with manipulation, read as mind-control. Many will resist the label of mind-control, but it cannot be denied that those who practice dark psychology tactics are able to follow a devious formula that provokes others to behave as the perpetrator wants. That is mind-control, but it may be more comfortable for some to label it as manipulation.

Manipulation comes in many forms, as mentioned in the previous chapter, where tactics were explored. What comes next is how those tactics do not exist in silos but rather mix and match to create common personality types that often fall into predictable categories. Some of these may seem obvious, while others may make you defensive, especially if you fall into one of these categories. The goal is not to vilify any of these people but rather to help you recognize that they may be manipulating you, whether to create positive or negative results, or to help you self-assess if you find you fit one or more of these categories. The term manipulator often has a negative connotation. When you hear "manipulator," you think, "bad person." But dare to open your mind just a bit and see how manipulation is not always intended for harm but can instead be a nudge that helps someone improve their life or choices or relationships. Bear that in mind as you keep reading.

Selfish People

Selfish people sound almost too common to include as part of this grouping, but it is truly connected to dark psychology. All you have to do is imagine someone you would describe as selfish who is or has been close to you personally. Now ask yourself what motivated their decision-making. The answer is obvious: their own benefit. This falls squarely into the Dark Triad under narcissism. Of course, a selfish person is not likely to warrant the label of narcissism, but they may have some traits in common. Recall that person again and ask yourself this time what they would do to get what they wanted. If you are able to list anything that involves lying, even white lies, then you can determine that they manipulated others to get what they want. If you can list any action that was done to make others feel bad or to take action for the person, then once again you can determine that they emotionally manipulated others to get what they want. This again connects to the Dark Triad under the label of Machiavellianism. A selfish person is often willing to "bend the truth" if it will benefit them. They will also engage in behaviors that get them attention or other desirable outcomes.

If you're struggling to think of an example for yourself, then use the example of a child who is spoiled. You could certainly say they were groomed to be selfish, but that does not change that some of the behaviors they engage in can be associated with dark psychology tactics. This can include the classic plot of crying to manipulate a parent's feelings. If the child gets what they want when they cry, they will continue to employ this tactic the next time they don't get their way. They may also use the tactic of love flooding by telling the parent they want to manipulate how much they love them and how important they are and how special. This is often followed by requests for something they want, and if they get it, they will have learned that this is another successful tactic to manipulate those around them.

This simplistic example is not all-inclusive, nor does it seek to vilify spoiled children. What it illustrates is how selfishness is connected to dark psychology, and subsequently dark psychology tactics.

Leaders

You may have done a double-take when reading this particular subtitle because, unlike manipulator, "leader" often has a strong positive association. After all, leaders are supposed to be those who guide us to greatness and make true and lasting change in the world. None of that is changed by what you will read next, but do not let your definition of leader prevent you from seeing how leaders use dark psychology.

A leader is often charismatic and engaging, so much so that they can convince others to do things they never thought possible. This all sounds great, but when you break it down, you can see the latent dark psychology at work. The first important part of that statement is the personality description. Charismatic and engaging are also descriptors associated with the Dark Triad personality types of a narcissist and Machiavellian. There is an undeniable magnetism in leaders, which is how they become leaders in the first place. The second important item in the initial statement is the word "convince." If someone has to convince you, that means they have to change your mind through what they say and do. In other words, mind-control. They make statements that get you to cry or laugh or nod in agreement. They act in ways that spur you to take action and work later or take on more responsibility because you want to please them or support them. The final important part of the first sentence is, "do things they never thought possible." That could be a source of inspiration from a leader. It could make you stop and think, "Wow, I never thought I could do that." However, that can also be a scary statement to make. You are admitting that another person was able to get you to do something you have never done before or may never have considered doing before. They got you to act out of character. That is a form of mind-control, manipulation, or inspiration. No matter which label you pick, there is still dark psychology at the root of it.

You may be left defeated by this section because you now feel you have failed by following strong leaders or even by becoming one. That is not true. What is true is that leadership can start with the best of intentions, an example of dark psychology being used for positive outcomes, but it may end with that same leader employing those successful tactics for outcomes that only suit their personal motivations. That is the lesson of this section. Do not dismiss all leaders as monsters but rather stop and analyze their statements, actions, tactics, allegiances, etc. before you commit to following them wholeheartedly. Be sure they have earned that trust.

Salespeople

You have likely already made the connection between sales and dark psychology, especially because it has already been mentioned in this book. Sales are driven by many factors, but the tactics used by salespeople are almost universally associated with dark psychology tactics.

It would be useless to list every single sales tactic, so, instead, we will explore one to help you build the connections on your own and then apply them to other scenarios as needed. The scenario we will look at is celebrity endorsement, an idea that has connections to John Broadus Watson.

The premise is obvious. First, you pick a celebrity. Next, you pick a product. Then you have that celebrity use the product, hold the product, and/or talk about the product in a positive way. While this may seem so obvious that you would never fall for such a dupe, stop and examine your own purchases. If you can name at least one product in your house that you automatically associate with a celebrity, then celebrity endorsement did its job. You do not even have to like the celebrity necessarily. What motivates you to buy the product is something else entirely.

Celebrity endorsements are so effective because they prey upon emotions. Emotional manipulation is more difficult to trace, and that is why it is one of the most utilized tactics in dark psychology. Many people would rather follow their "instincts" than to follow a straightforward and logical path. Ultimately, most people trust themselves above all others. With a celebrity endorsement, salespeople are drawing a connection between a product and a successful person. Now when you see that product, you think of the celebrity. When you think of "celebrity," you think of success. When you think of success, you think of how you want it. You may look back at the product and think of how you are smart enough to be as successful as that celebrity, and maybe, just maybe, if you use that same product, you will get to success sooner. Maybe you think it will make you look like that celebrity or act like that celebrity. This feeds into your fantasies about being someone more than who you are. Who wouldn't want to feel as skilled/beautiful/smart as someone others admire? Society's fascination with celebrity makes this an easy win for salespeople looking for a quick way to catch your attention and teach you to associate them and their product with someone the world has put on a pedestal.

This is only one of many examples of how salespeople use manipulative tactics to make sales. To find out if you are falling prey to your emotions rather than following reason and logic, take a step back. Why do you want the product? What immediate positive effect will it have on your life? Is it truly useful, or does it serve as more of a status symbol? Impulse buying is real, so do not get drawn into a purchase because you are unable to see the dark psychology at work.

Lawyers

Lawyers can do immense good, but they can also do immense harm. The ways in which they accomplish both are nearly identical, and they often find their source in dark psychology.

Whether you have been directly involved in a criminal proceeding or not, it is not difficult to see the ways in which dark psychology can keep justice from being blind. That is because lawyers are speaking to humans, and humans are fallible beings. Humans are also the only living things who have dark psychology hardwired into them. It is no surprise that a lawyer would use this innate ability to their advantage in court.

As with our other subtopics, imagine a scenario. A trial is being held for murder. The evidence is presented, the jury reaches a verdict, and the defendant is declared guilty. The prosecutor has successfully won the case. Then a technicality allows the defense to call for a mistrial. Everything starts over. The same evidence is presented, the jury reaches a verdict, but this time the defendant is declared not guilty. This seems ludicrous. After all, if the evidence did not change, the verdict should remain stable. The answer should be clear. However, it still happened, so the next step is to determine how and why.

The how is not difficult to pinpoint. The defense lawyer most likely used dark psychology tactics to come at the jury in new and more convincing ways. After all, they had the first trial to see what worked and what did not. Now, they have a new opportunity to try a different angle. Again, the evidence did not change. The lawyer simply presented it in a new way. This could be as simple as adjusting their tone or changing their phrasing. However, these subtle changes can reap massive results if the jury is susceptible to these dark psychology tactics. The lawyer only needs to produce reasonable doubt, so if they can flip their words around in such a way that they plant the seed of doubt in the jury, then that seed is left to grow into a not guilty verdict.

What you need to recognize in this scenario is the why. Why did the verdict change? It changed because one lawyer more successfully manipulated the jury than the other. The jury, for whatever reason, felt the need to side with the defense. Notice the word "felt" in that sentence. It is very intentional because it points to how emotions cannot be entirely removed from human decisions, even in something as high stakes as a murder trial. Impartial is practically impossible. Everyone will come with a bias, so all the lawyer has to do is successfully manipulate those biases to be amplified or muted when someone makes their decision. This is also why the most successful lawyers are not known for how they find key evidence or present a logical case. Those may be factors in their success, but they are more often known for being able to play to the jury, question witnesses, or present powerful opening and closing statements. Their ability to play with words, and therefore play with emotions, is what makes them good, and it is also what makes them practitioners of dark psychology.

Politicians

This section may have some nodding their heads in agreement or others cringing and thinking about skipping this section. You should continue anyway because this is an all-encompassing discussion of politicians, not one which takes a particular side.

First, stop and think about the definition of a politician. They are intended to be a public servant, someone who serves the interests of the people, their constituents. Next, think about what a politician does. They make decisions that impact others, including themselves, and argue how those decisions are in the best interest of their constituents. So far, this may sound like a lesson on government, but stop and break down the who and the what behind a politician.

A politician is a person, perhaps a person you could say is just like any other. This could be true, but what you may be leaving out of your assessment is the plain and simple fact that politicians are public figures. Public means they are put on display for all to see. But not at all times. Politicians have carefully planned schedules. They know where they are going, who they will be seeing and talking to, and who will be watching them. That means they are able to curate themselves. The use of the word curate is meant to draw attention to how politicians craft a public persona. They would have you believe that the person you watch on television is the same person you would casually meet on the street. More often than not, that is a lie. After all, think of the countless scandals that have ruined a politician. The public is frequently shocked by such revelations. The politician would not have ruined their career and/or reputation if the public already knew they were the kind of person who engaged in such behavior. You may also be thinking of many politicians who survived after such scandals. They survive such scandals because they were so successful in convincing their constituents with their persona that the public chooses to overlook those misdeeds in favor of the persona they bought into. Therefore, the who behind a politician is often misleading, as it is a carefully manufactured and planned creation, not an actual human being who behaves in those ways at all times.

A politician is engaged in decision-making, and as such, they are privileged with a certain amount of authority and power. Recall the experiment explored earlier in which a group of people entered a fake jailhouse as peers but quickly succumbed to the power of labels. Those who were labeled as an authority began to engage in uncharacteristic and disturbing behaviors. This is not to say that all people in power will be corrupted by that power, but it does mean you should pause and evaluate thoroughly how that power is being wielded. You should also assess if the power is being used consistently. A politician's power means other, less powerful people will be drawn to them. This places them in a prime situation to become victims if the politician chooses to be a perpetrator. A politician's power means others with power, often those with more power, will try to manipulate that politician into using their power for the other's benefit. It quickly becomes a tangled web of complicated motivations and allegiances. What is most notable, however, is that all of these power dynamics are made possible because the person with power allows that label to indeed place them above those who are powerless. After all, there are plenty of politicians whose constituents may voice their opinion to vote to pass a bill or law, but the politician votes against it. When this occurs, then you have to dig deeper into what the politician does versus what they are supposed to do. They are making decisions, but how consistently do those decisions align with the cares and concerns of the people they claim to represent. You may or may not be surprised to find that nearly every single one has voted contrary to their constituents' demands at least once. That is because they are human, and they are often engaging in the use of dark psychology.

It is easy to see now how a politician is set up to be a devotee to dark psychology. Their persona is in line with both characteristics of a narcissist and a Machiavellian. Their motivations, whether personal or political, can also be tied to Machiavellianism or psychopathy. You could even argue that politicians, along with most others in positions of extreme power, will almost always fit into one or more of these personality types within the Dark Triad. This is not to say all politicians will engage in such behaviors, but it should make you pause and examine how and why they became a politician in the first place and who benefits from their decisions. It could be a dark journey, but it is much more satisfying to understand how they may be engaging in mind-control practices than to unwittingly fall for their carefully laid traps. Never fear to question. Questioning can lead you to discoveries that keep you safe from the circle of victimization created by the most sinister perpetrators.

Analyzing Motivation

This chapter shows you the ease with which a common person may, in fact, be using dark psychology for nefarious purposes. You may also be questioning how many of your decisions are truly good versus motivated by the propensity for dark psychology that lies in all of use. Here are a few questions to help you break down yours and others' decisions to discover the true motivation.

1. Why did you initiate this action or interaction?
2. Who does this benefit directly in the short-term and in the long-term?
3. How much, if at all, did you "stretch the truth" in your interaction?
4. Is what you're saying designed to build a stronger relationship with those you are interacting with?
5. Is your approach to the situation based on the desire for mutually positive outcomes?

This is not an exhaustive list, of course, but it is a great way to guide your thought process as you analyze motivations and strategies that may be at play in your life. No one can be expected to avoid dark psychology entirely. As has been stated previously, it is entirely human to have thoughts and take actions that are designed to victimize others. What is being asked of you and of everyone is that actions are not taken without self-reflection. These questions also prompt you to reach a new level of awareness. Note that the word is "awareness," not "paranoia." These questions are not something you should have to visit daily but only when you are in a more dangerous and serious situation. Beyond that, they may be a fun exercise to analyze ways you may have succumbed to a salesperson's tactics, for example, but that is not the goal. The goal is to put the power back in your hands and leave you feeling empowered to understand the dark psychology at play all around you.

CHAPTER 6
The Dark Side Of Dark Psychology

You will encounter dark psychology tactics on a daily basis. That is inevitable. What is far less likely is that you will be pulled to the darkest end of the Dark Continuum. As you may recall from the chapter on dark psychology terms, the Dark Continuum is a spectrum with which to measure how close someone's behavior approaches true evil. This deeply dark end of the spectrum, a place where absolute evil exists, is known as the Dark Singularity. Of course, it is difficult to define what "pure evil" means, but it is not too hard to see how many notorious figures throughout history can fall on the darker end of the Dark Continuum. These are the nightmarish individuals whose motivations often cannot be found and whose actions defy what we understand to be within the scope of human possibility. These are the people you would call inhuman, calculating, ruthless, and chaotic. This chapter is a look into what it means to take dark psychology too far and yet how the darkness of only one perpetrator can still pull in a massive number of victims.

Breaking Down the Dark Terms

Before you can properly understand the dark psychology behind the darkest of criminals, you have to understand some dark terms that will help guide you. The Dark Continuum is first. This continuum does not have a set beginning but does have a set end. You could think of the beginning as mere thoughts of victimizing someone for no clear evolutionary purpose. It could be a fleeting desire, but it still falls on that spectrum. From an action point of view, you could think of the beginning as the impulse to violently strike out as a gut reaction to someone doing something you do not like. At that moment, all you want to do is kick, hit, punch, but you do not. At this end, you are still in control and are still self-aware enough to stop yourself from engaging in dark behavior. Some of the stops along this continuum would be many of the personality types we have discussed. A selfish person who is relatively harmless would be low on the continuum. A manipulative leader with Machiavellian tendencies would be further along. Anyone who has a personality type that closely aligns with those of the Dark Triad would be even further up. Those who possess elements of all three personality types of the Dark Triad are beginning to approach the end of the continuum.

The end of the Dark Continuum is defined as the Dark Singularity, the pit of inhumane and unfathomable behavior. It may be tempting to place many famous criminals' acts on the end of the Dark Continuum, but that is very difficult, if not impossible, to achieve. That is not to say that those who approach this end are worthy of sympathy or even forgiveness but to illustrate that these individuals often have other contributing factors that have placed them closer to the Dark Singularity.

This leads us to the term Dark Factor. Dark Factor is a measure of how likely someone is to engage in dark behavior and to use dark psychology tactics when interacting with others. Dark Factor is not something you can claim a person has had since birth, but you can make the claim that the Dark Factor is stronger in some individuals than in others. Some of the experiences that could increase someone's Dark Factor include an abusive childhood, neglect, an abusive relationship, a traumatic event, a traumatic injury (often a head injury), and more. Some readers may find themselves bristling at this list because they have experienced some of these traumas or someone they love has and is a completely decent and wonderful human being. That is possible, maybe even more likely. However, that does not negate the fact that these triggers can take someone who was already without a conscience and push them into behaviors that approach the Dark Singularity. Connecting these events to these behaviors is also what can enable us to detect these individuals before they get out of control. It is a matter of seeing the warning signs and using them to understand where a person's behavior may go next.

Once a person's Dark Factor is taken into account, then their level of Darkness Manipulation comes into play. Darkness Manipulation is a person's ability to use dark psychology tactics effectively. Someone may have a large amount of Dark Factor, fall within the Dark Triad, and settle on the dark end of the Dark Continuum but still not be a successful criminal or manipulator. That is because their Darkness Manipulation is not as masterful as others. It is not a matter of knowing the tactics but of knowing how and when to use them. A strategy such as gift giving, or withdrawal, is an effective tactic only if the perpetrator has chosen something that will motivate the victim to behave as desired. If the perpetrator chooses the wrong tactic to victimize, they will fail at their manipulation and get caught. This could mean that their Dark Factor is stunted by the criminal justice system because they were caught early in their darkness development. It could also mean that their failure will teach them, and their Darkness Manipulation will only increase with time. There is no set formula for how this will work out, but it is important to recognize all of these nuances at play and how they tie in together to create a person who may come dangerously close to the Dark Singularity.

Historical Dark Manipulators

The list of dark manipulators throughout time would be extensive indeed, so this list is meant to be a brief exposure that uses some well-known examples. Well-known examples are still relevant because they will help you take your prior knowledge and combine it with your new knowledge about dark psychology. This will give you a fresh and valuable perspective about how and why certain dark figures were able to come to power and to such devastating effect.

Our first historical figure is **Al Capone**. Not everyone may be interested in Mob related history, but Al Capone is a worthy subject for study because of the traceable dark factors and dark tactics that directly contributed to his criminal life.

The first factor at play is Al Capone's childhood. From a young age, he became involved in gang violence. This is how he suffered a facial injury that resulted in the nickname "Scarface." It is likely that he was drawn into the gangs through the use of rudimentary dark psychology tactics. A gang could offer protection and a sense of belonging. These are tempting enticements for a child who may not have had a sense of safety or belonging before. This is a kind of base-level brainwashing. A younger person is more susceptible, of course, which means they are drawn in and stay in because they've never known anything else. This initiation into crime and criminal thinking is a clear indicator that raises Al Capone's Dark Factor. He was likely taught how to use moral disengagement to compartmentalize his conscience from his actions whenever necessary. Instead of seeing the negative impact of his actions, he saw the benefits it would bring him and the gang who had welcomed him. That would make it much easier to frequently engage in criminal acts without any pangs of remorse. Without those early experiences, it is unclear when or if he would have turned to his life of organized crime.

The next noteworthy strategy in Al Capone's history was his use of Machiavellian tactics to groom politicians and media associates into believing he was a good guy. He created a persona that drew in these people and led them to believe his intentions were ultimately in the best interest of everyone. His lies and charisma drew them in and kept them in line with what would most benefit him and his criminal allies. As he learned from his early experiences, it does not take much to draw someone in if they are craving attention, belonging, or safety. Those motivations would entice dozens of people to also morally disengage and somehow believe that aiding and abetting Al Capone was the right thing to do. That is an obvious portrait of someone using dark psychology on a regular basis and with selfish intentions. This careful manipulation is perhaps part of why gang violence at the time escalated to new heights before anyone attempted to take down Al Capone. Even now, he is a fascinating figure who is the center of many films, books, and TV show adaptations. His charm is still convincing people to almost idolize him. His name is known, for better or for worse, because of the ways in which he used dark psychology to build his criminal empire.

Another notorious individual who plagues the minds of society at large is **Jeffrey Dahmer**. If you are unfamiliar with his crimes, he engaged in kidnapping, torture, rape, mutilation, murder, and cannibalism of young men and boys. His crimes fall on the very dark end of the Dark

Continuum and would rank among those crimes deemed inhuman by many. Although you may feel you can never reach an understanding of why this behavior occurred, you can benefit from understanding how the Dark Factor in Jeffrey Dahmer's life built up over time and led into the explosive and violent behavior he displayed later in life.

As with many serial killers, Jeffrey Dahmer's childhood is a potential and likely source for why his Dark Factor reached such substantial heights and brought him so close to the Dark Singularity. Interviews and books by Dahmer's parents do not point to obvious sources for his eventual deviant behaviors, but it only takes a moment to read between the lines and find them.

First, his parents were not deeply involved in his life from a young age. Their marriage was tenuous, and so they devoted themselves to other things, often leaving Dahmer to himself. This isolation meant he was left unchecked and could develop antisocial behaviors without early or strategic intervention. Since his parents' marriage was unhappy, he frequently witnessed verbal altercations between them, which may have made him wary of romantic relationships and unsure of how to develop positive relationships.

When his parents did get divorced finally, his isolation increased because his mother and brother left, ending contact with him, and his father was disengaged from him. At this time, some deviant behaviors that pointed to psychopathy began to show. He started finding dead animals, collecting their carcasses, and then mutilating them to create startling displays. This kind of cry for help left him to fall deeper and deeper into the psychopathic tendencies he already possessed.

This shows his connection to the Dark Triad, a psychopath who lacks empathy and a conscience. Couple this with his inability to create positive social relationships, and you are left with the undeniable chaos that created his violent and unpredictable behavior. Another indicator of his psychopathy was the fact that he described his desire to kidnap, torture, rape, kill, and cannibalize as a compulsion. Dark psychology lacks an evolutionary motive, and that is certainly true in the case of Jeffrey Dahmer.

The next figure we will analyze is John Wayne Gacy, Jr. He, like Dahmer, was a psychopath who was likely drawn into criminal behavior by a difficult childhood. Of course, not every serial killer has a terrible childhood, and not everyone who has a terrible childhood will become a serial killer. What is relevant is how we can use an understanding of dark psychology and the Dark Factor to see how and why Gacy developed into such a disturbing murderer. For those who may be unfamiliar with his story, he is often referred to as the "Killer Clown" and was responsible for the rape, torture, and murder of a large number of young men and boys over a period of six years and buried them beneath his home.

Gacy's descent on the Dark Continuum can be connected to his father. His father was an alcoholic who also subscribed to the misogynistic view that every young boy should engage exclusively in "manly" pursuits, like sports and hunting and outdoor activities. Instead, Gacy preferred cooking and gardening and other activities that would be deemed too "girly" by his father. Gacy was constantly disappointing his father in this way, and his father made his disappointment clear. This meant Gacy repressed these behaviors and therefore repressed his homosexuality. He buried this part of his identity in an attempt to please his father.

At this point, Gacy may seem like the victim, but what comes next shows a shift from victim to perpetrator. His first victims were his family and community. He was so intent on denying his homosexuality that he first convinced a woman to marry him and start a family with him. He may have been pushed to hate his homosexuality, but he made a conscious choice to find a wife and manufacture a life that would be approved by his father. This was only the beginning of his lies.

After he fixed himself as the devoted husband and father, he slipped and was found guilty of sodomizing a young boy. He was convicted and incarcerated. While incarcerated, his father died, which is perhaps the stimulus that pushed him into a deeper spiral down the Dark Continuum. He felt that perhaps it was his conviction that made his father die of shame and humiliation. Gacy then made it his mission to be an even more convincing "upstanding" figure. He started a business and became a fixture in the community who was well-known and liked. Here is the foundation for his dark psychology. He created a world based entirely on lies. What motivated him was his desire to convince others that he was an entirely different person. This Machiavellian mentality was immensely successful.

This leads us to the most disturbing and sinister part of his development along the Dark Continuum. Gacy created a character called Pogo the Clown. He would dress as a clown and perform at children's parties and other community gatherings. His Darkness Manipulation, especially when performing as Pogo, was absurdly powerful. Parents were willing to entrust their children to him. They would even encourage their children to play with Pogo. Gacy had found the perfect persona that would draw in his prey and their parents alike. It would be incredibly difficult to suspect evil would come from a businessman who is deeply involved in the community and plays a harmless clown. That is exactly what made his Darkness Manipulation so skillful. He had the draw of a narcissist, the lying capabilities of a Machiavellian, and the lack of empathy of a psychopath. His Dark Factor became so rooted in the Dark Triad that it is not difficult to see how he came so close to the Dark Singularity.

An undeniable connection exists between dark psychology and cults. Cult leaders are extremely adept at using dark psychology tactics to attract followers and to keep them committed against their better judgment. That is why we will next look at **Charles Manson**. Charles Manson is known for his "family" of followers and the shocking murders that they committed in the late sixties.

There is no need to dig too deeply into Charles Manson's childhood, although there it does point to how his Dark Factor could have developed from a young age. His mother was a sex worker and alcoholic who eventually abandoned him by the age of twelve. He was left to find his own way, and that may have been a contributing factor in his development as a devious and manipulative individual.

Charles Manson eventually decided that he should form the Manson Family, a group of people who enjoyed the use of LSD and psychedelic mushrooms and who also committed to believing that Manson was a new Messiah who had prophetic visions. You may be shaking your head in disbelief at this point. Who could be so delusional that they would fall for such a scheme? That is where the majority of dark psychology tactics come into play.

The initial tactic used by most cult leaders is charisma and ego, the classic narcissist. The cult leader will appear to be immensely charming and engaging, someone who it feels like can speak to your very soul. The cult leader so strongly believes in themselves that the followers believe it, too. The followers have often never known such confidence, so when someone is so self-assured and enticing, the followers fall in love, not necessarily with the leader, but with the persona they present. It is an intoxicating blend of kindness, charm, and confidence that is hard to resist when your defenses are down.

One of the key tactics utilized by nearly every cult leader is isolation. Cult leaders know that if they separate a person from their support system, the only one they can turn to is the cult leader. It creates a dangerous dependence on the cult leader. Cult leaders also know that it is easier to isolate someone who is in need emotionally. Those who are depressed or anxious or lonely will be drawn in by the opportunity to belong to a community that welcomes them. It is likely that the cult leader will then engage in love flooding and compliments and gift giving as a way to show the person how generous the leader is and how caring. Once the follower is immersed in this codependent relationship, then the cult leader can resort to the crueler tactics, such as threatening withdrawal and love denial. Then the follower will find themselves rejected from the community and with no one to help them because they have isolated themselves so completely from the outside world and outside support. The only choice is the cult leader.

Cult leaders like Manson are also talented at brainwashing. This includes the social-isolation described above as well as fatigue-inducement and starvation. When the followers are not allowed to sleep, and it is the cult leader who is withholding sleep, they will often do whatever is asked of them in order to finally sleep. The same is done with food. In the case of Manson, he also used hallucinatory substances to convince his family that he had prophetic visions. The mental states of his family members were in total disarray, which left them open to complete and total mind-control.

Manson's use of Dark Manipulation was so skilled that he never actually committed a murder. He did not commit the murders, but he was able to convince multiple people to go out multiple times to kill others. This level of mind-control is difficult to understand. Few people believe themselves capable of murder without any clear motivation, but dark psychology made it possible for Manson to control his followers and coerce them into behaving in uncharacteristic and violent ways. His control was so absolute that, even as they faced the death penalty, his followers would sing and giggle and make faces throughout the trial process. Their minds became the playgrounds in which he lived out his grandiose fantasies of power and prestige, a true practitioner of dark psychology.

These historical examples only begin to scrape the surface of the depravity that exists in many criminals. However, it does show that the Dark Continuum is vast. With enough Dark Factor and enough skill with Darkness Manipulation, it is possible to come incredibly close to the Dark Singularity. When you hear about the next notorious criminal who lands in the spotlight, trace back through their personal history and see if you can find the signs and detect where they put dark psychology to work before they were finally stopped.

CHAPTER 7
Dark Psychology And Social Media

Nearly every modern person of a certain age is guilty of connecting their lives to social media, whether it is through Facebook, Instagram, Twitter, Snapchat, or YouTube. We are constantly plugged into a stream of media that is ever-changing and highly engaging. The world wide web is at the tips of your fingers at nearly every minute of every day. However, there is latent darkness at work behind social media. The internet opened a vast portal into knowledge and connection, but it also created a highly convenient and exploitable method for perpetrators to find and harass more victims. This chapter is meant to dive into how social media can be a hotbed of dark predators whose posts and responses employ a variety of dark psychology tactics that have real-world consequences. After all, what predator would shy away from being a faceless entity in a virtual world? Anonymity is the perfect cloak for someone whose sole purpose is to victimize those around them.

How Social Media Invites the Darkness

When social media first began, the intent was to allow people to stay in contact, to feel more involved with friends' lives, and to put on display whatever part of our lives we most wanted to show. That initial intent was perhaps good, but the way in which it has evolved has left a huge opening for dark predators.

Social media is susceptible to Dark Manipulators first and foremost because it is so easy to be anonymous. The plethora of various usernames and account profiles are nothing more or less than what the user makes of them. They can be from anywhere, like anything, change age, gender, nationality, and more, all with the click of a few buttons and the typing of a few words. There are hundreds upon hundreds of profiles that are closer to being characters than they are to being human beings. This idea has a profound connection to narcissism and egoism. The difference is the person who is at the center of narcissism or egoism may not be a person at all but is instead a fantasy person created by a perpetrator. This makes them free to be whatever they want, even if the person they create acts in ways they never would in real life.

Social media, in many ways, encourages narcissism because your posts are intended to generate attention for yourself, whether positive or negative. It is difficult to argue that a post can truly be selfless when your name is always attached to what you post. Even reposting someone else's content is, in a way, showing support for whatever that content is. You want anyone who follows you to understand that you like and support that content so much that you want others to see it. The content is irrelevant when you look at social media from this angle. You could try to argue for days that your intent was to start a positive conversation or to make someone smile, but it all ultimately points back to you. You wanted something, some kind of response, and your post gave you what you wanted. That could be satisfaction at spreading an idea you support or the simple joy of having others like what you have to say. The motivation is always tied up in how it reflects back on the user. This is an addicting setup because you can place yourself on stage but let other people technically decide whether they want to pay attention. It makes you feel like you are less of a performer on social media, but the fact is everyone is performing on social media. They are performing whatever version of themselves that they want the world to see, understand, and interact with. That is why so many posts are designed to provoke likes or retweets or even negative responses. The performer ultimately wants to know someone is watching the performance.

Dark Manipulators also flock to social media because it is a platform that allows you to say highly inflammatory things and be admired for it. There are countless posts which many people would never dare say as a statement made to another person, and yet those posts are put up and interacted with again and again. The fact that you do not have to see the person on the other side allows you to more readily use moral disengagement. The profile you are viewing does not feel like a person, so you can justify that it is okay to say something much harsher than you would in person. You morally disengage actual reality from virtual reality and decide that each level of existence has its own unique morality. When you look at it that way, it is obvious how social media invites the influences of dark psychology. It is almost a fantasy world in which you can say whatever you want and show whatever you want and still go out into reality and act in completely different ways. This is also perhaps why many people will spend their time together still glued to a screen. They are no longer interested in interacting in reality as much as they are interested in interacting with their virtual reality. Just as we discussed the way a politician curates their self-image, that is precisely what you do when you create and use a social media profile. This is inherently Machiavellian. You are lying to show only those parts of yourself that will benefit you. Even if you post something unflattering and then talk about working on yourself, you are asking whoever views that post to give you attention, to celebrate you or support you. That makes you feel good, and that is enough of a motivation to call what you are doing Machiavellian and narcissistic. Lying to manipulate and centering yourself is at the heart of social media. That is already two-thirds of the Dark Triad.

Once anonymity and facelessness are established, the next dark temptation is to act on impulse. Social media posts are like a live film, constantly evolving within the moment and completely uncensored. If too much time passes, the momentum is lost, and the post may lose steam. Therefore, social media invites impulsivity and chaos. There is no time for reflection after the initial post. What happens next is in real-time, so you have to post now or miss out. There is an addiction to staying on top of the latest trends or the latest news, so waiting would leave you behind. Since you have to act quickly, you are robbed of the time it would take to think through what you are going to say, how you are going to say it, and whether you should be saying anything at all. Within that moment, you are being invited to take the fleeting thoughts related to dark psychology and perform them live, right now, without thought. Social media almost demands that you post your initial gut reaction, fraught with intense emotion, and full of uncharacteristic vitriol. That is how you bring in the last part of the Dark Triad. A psychopath has no conscience, lacks empathy, and moves with impulsivity. You are not necessarily a psychopathic personality generally, but social media drives you to act in psychopathic ways. You set morality and reason aside to react at that instant rather than miss out on the chance to stay involved in whatever is happening. This causes users to speak and act in ways that are not connected to the reality of who they are. When you respond to a post at that moment, you have not taken the time to think about the other person's reaction beyond the thought that you want them to react. You do not consider their perspective in a humane way but only as a way to gauge how successful you were with your own posting practices. You also cannot engage your conscience if you respond at that precise moment. You are not thinking through whether it is "right" or "wrong" but rather whether it will be well-received or frequently noticed. Attention is attention, whether positive or negative, so you dive into the chaos of impulsive posting. You have behaved as a psychopath may. Now the Dark Triad in social media is complete.

Dark Social Media Types

The first part of this chapter shows the ways in which the internet, and specifically social media, create a breeding ground for dark psychology and all that it entails. This section is an exploration of some of the types of social media abusers and what each of them does to create victims. It is important to establish that these actions, although done in a virtual setting, have real-life implications. The victim is no less victimized because what they are experiencing is happening online rather than face to face. The perpetrators are also no less dangerous because they are far away and faceless. The danger is real, so read on to learn more about the most common dark social media types.

You may already be familiar with the term **keyboard warrior**, but you may not fully understand what it has to do with dark psychology. First, a keyboard warrior is defined as someone who initiates intense virtual interactions to defend or promote a particular viewpoint. A keyboard warrior has deeply entrenched beliefs that are at the heart of every post and comment they make. This may not sound terrible at first. After all, someone who has strong convictions can often be appealing or admirable. What is dangerous, however, is when the beliefs they subscribe to are harmful are downright misinformed. What is also dangerous is when they believe something positive, but are so determined to beat their opposers down, that they go too far.

Keyboard warriors will most often engage in dark psychology tactics that are verbal since, as the name implies, they are only able to type rather than take physical action. One typical example would be semantic manipulation. A keyboard warrior will word something in such a way that the meaning can be manipulated. This is a trap for whoever responds to the keyboard warrior because then the keyboard warrior can instantly fight back and claim that the responder misunderstood what they were saying. This gives the predator a twofold victory. First, they controlled their victim's response, and second, they undermined their victim's authority by making them sound inept at understanding what the perpetrator has to say. It is a vicious cycle that can go back and forth and even cause the victim/perpetrator dynamic to be flipped if two keyboard warriors decided to engage in the discussion. There can even be collectives of keyboard warriors who work in conjunction with one another, creating a pack-mentality that also encourages uncharacteristic behavior and increases animosity towards others.

Keyboard warriors will also engage in dark psychology tactics that seem positive to other users and make them take the side of the perpetrator. They may try to use love flooding in a virtual way by liking comments that are supportive of them or excessively praising those who reinforce what the keyboard warrior is saying. This makes those responders feel validated and valued, so they are more likely to defend the keyboard warrior even as they devolve into more heated and perhaps aggressive rants. This is almost like the creation of a virtual cult. The leader, the keyboard warrior, has a curated persona that is strong and confident that others flock to. Once that initial charm has drawn someone in, it becomes easier and easier to use moral disengagement to separate the virtual from the real. Then the keyboard warrior has a following, a group of fellow virtual devotees who will rush to defend and aid their leader. Online communities have the same risk factors as those in real life.

Another dark social media type is the **cyberbully**. Bullies have been a constant concern for families and young people for decades. They are self-appointed predators who often victimize others to make themselves feel more important or to distract from their own problems. Before the internet, these bullies were much easier to track because they had to interact with someone in person in order to bully. There was a concrete action or a concrete statement that could be witnessed and documented and punished as needed. The internet, however, has given them a chance to be anonymous and faceless and has extended their victim pool to include anyone, not just those within their immediate social circle or community. It also does not require any level of physical intimidation. A cyberbully intimidates because of what they say much more than what they do. This means they engage in emotional bullying, which is much more damaging psychologically. A bruise can heal, but the comments a cyberbully makes have made an emotional impression on the victim that is not a visible wound.

A cyberbully may sound like something insubstantial, but there is a characteristic of cyberbullying that makes its marks even more lasting. Once something has been posted on social media, it is there for the world to see and often there forever. There are some regulations on social media sites now that allow others to report harmful comments or content, but that does not stop dozens or even hundreds of people from seeing it and perhaps screenshotting it for later. This means that the cyberbully's words do not disappear after they are said but are there to be read and experienced again and again and again. This means the victim cannot walk away from the experience after the cyberbully has made their statement but instead must revisit that feeling every time they see the post or others mention the post. This can keep the victim in a constant cycle of anxiety and self-consciousness that is crippling. That is why cyberbullying is potentially even worse than in-person bullying. The perpetrator is harder to find, and what the perpetrator does is practically immortalized on the internet for years to come. It is also possible for a cyberbully to move their bullying off of mainstream social media and onto alternative platforms that may even encourage and support their behavior. The cyberbully can keep on bullying the victim, perhaps without the victim's knowledge, but the cyberbully can still get a sadistic satisfaction out of watching their victim be victimized again by others on other platforms.

A cyberbully is most likely to fall under the label of narcissist or Machiavellian. They can be narcissists because they are attention-seeking. By making the victim seem lesser, they, in turn, seem more important or better. They also want everything to point back to them, and cyberbullying makes them feel superior because they were able to bring down their victim. They can be considered Machiavellian because they can easily post lies with impunity. There is no fact-check button that can be pressed on social media. The cyberbully has the ability to make up whatever lie they want about the victim. They can also tailor their lies to the victim by first analyzing the victim's profile. Their analysis can help them pinpoint the victim's weaknesses and therefore make their lies more strategic. They will know how to provoke the exact response that suits their needs.

The final dark social media type we will explore is the **cyberstalker**. A cyberstalker is someone who uses the internet to track someone. This is not quite the same as a real-life stalker. A cyberstalker can be almost undetectable if they wish. What they are interested in is following the victim, and if the cyberstalker has created a convincing profile, that is easy to do on social media.

Social media is not entirely about posts. It also includes pictures. This is what a cyberstalker would most want to see. If the victim shares their location or mentions that they always go to a certain place, then the cyberstalker has the knowledge to find you in real life if they want. They can use the backgrounds of your photos to pinpoint what parks you visit, what stores you shop in, what theaters you frequent, what school you or your kids attend. Those photos can tell them immense amounts of information about you and your daily life. For example, many apps can be used to track your exercises, such as a running route. It is likely you or someone you know has posted their run before with the time circled because they achieved a personal record. This has the appearance of being a great celebration for someone's achievement, but to a cyberstalker, it is a literal map of where to find you and possibly even when you run, if that was included in the picture posted.

Cyberstalkers are perhaps the most concerning dark social media type. If they choose to stalk you but do not engage with your social media profiles, you could be stalked and never know it. The only way you may find out is if the cyberstalker decides to bring their stalking practices to reality. They may also be following you in other ways than only on social media. If you have left your accounts vulnerable, they may be tracking your emails or apps and use them to gain sensitive information about your personal life. They will dig into whatever part of your life they can get to if it is available on the internet. They are also menacing because they can always change profiles or names if you do detect them. Be wary of who you accept into your social media circles. If someone has victimized you before, it is likely they will seek to victimize you repeatedly, if they can.

This chapter may sound like a massive, dire warning about the ills of social media, but before you go delete all of your accounts, stop and think. There are responsible ways to use the internet and social media that do not have to stray into the Dark Continuum.

What you need to do is start with yourself. Think about your own profile and what it contains. Ask yourself why you post certain things or why you respond to certain people. What are your motivations? What is your goal? Does your profile truly show who you are as a person? Does what you say virtually match what you say in real life? The goal is to make virtual reality and true reality as close to the same as possible. This can ensure that you are always acting within the boundaries of your moral character and will make you actively engage in the empathetic practices you would use in face-to-face interactions.

The next step is to think before you post. It is so tempting to fall into the instant gratification of typing a response at that exact moment. However, that is exactly how you allow the dark psychology at work within you to become a prominent part of who you are instead of a merely human tendency that you do not indulge. Stop and think about what you will say, how you will say it, and whether you should respond in the first place. Evaluate if you are just making yourself a target for a keyboard warrior and are starting an argument you never wanted to be part of. More often than not, you will find it's not worth it. It is much healthier to walk away. Dark psychology is not all bad, but giving in to your dark tendencies without careful care and consideration can pull you to a place on the Dark Continuum where you never wanted to be.

The final step to ensure you do not fall into the dark traps of social media is to protect your accounts. Make sure you are only inviting people into your social circle that you trust. If you do allow most people to follow you, then be deliberate with what you post and how much you share about your life. Ask yourself if what you are sharing would make a better conversation piece for your friend's dinner table than for everyone who follows you on social media. Take the photos of your favorite haunts and make a genuine album rather than one on social media. That will prevent you from giving too much of yourself away and will help you re-engage with reality. Do not make yourself an easy target for a predator. Show them that you will not be made the victim and that your awareness of dark psychology tactics has equipped you to see them coming before they can do you harm.

CHAPTER 8
Deviant Behavior And Dark Psychology

Dark psychology is a never-ending maze of nuances and terms, but it may be intriguing to you to know how dark psychology is a latent factor in a large number of criminal behaviors and labels. After all, the goal of most criminals is to achieve something for themselves by making a victim out of someone else. Few crimes are completely disconnected from other people and more often are committed because of how they affect other people. Once again, the dynamic of dark psychology is dependent on the relationship between the perpetrator and the victim. Notice that these terms have been used throughout this text but that they are also terms regularly used in law enforcement. That is not a coincidence. Dark psychology and criminality have a strong connection, and that is especially true of certain kinds of criminals.

Criminal Labels

There are many kinds of criminal labels, such as robber or money launderer. These are not people we would want to encounter or people we would enjoy, but those labels do not spark the same level of fear as some others do. There is an implication behind each label that leads us to make judgments about what level of criminal someone could be. This is our own attempt to place them on the Dark Continuum in such a way that satisfies our understanding of others' depravity.

One criminal label that is commonly used is a **sociopath**. Do not confuse sociopaths with psychopaths. A psychopath has no conscience, lacks empathy, and acts on impulse. A sociopath, on the other hand, has a limited conscience and lacks empathy. Their limited conscience means they can fully understand if something is wrong and choose to do it anyway. It is also important to note that this is a clinical diagnosis and not something a layperson can use to describe a person without that official diagnosis. If you are unsure of which term may be appropriate, it is much better to avoid trying to label someone at all. It is tempting to describe someone you may know with such a strong diagnosis, but that is unfair to the individual and reduces the impact that these are a medical diagnosis and not simply titles created to describe certain people. These labels bear an immense wait and should not be taken lightly.

Sociopaths are almost harder to fathom than psychopaths because they do have a concept of what a conscience is. A true psychopath is not able to conceptualize right or wrong, so it is easier to see how they commit terrible crimes. A sociopath, however, is able to understand but goes through with their criminal acts anyway. They can almost seem like any other fully functioning human, except the fact that they can set aside morality and commit any number of crimes. They may know it is wrong, but they may not understand why it matters that it is wrong. Perhaps what is more important, then, is that they do not have the ability to empathize. If they cannot understand how their actions will cause someone pain or sadness or anger, etc., then you can begin to understand why they could move forward with their immoral act. They know it is wrong, but they do not see the consequences that the action will have on the victim emotionally. They are unable to rationalize how someone may react to the negative stimulus of something they do.

Sociopaths are also known to be antisocial. This does not mean that they avoid all social interactions, but rather that the interactions they do have, go against typical, acceptable behaviors when interacting with others. These individuals, when encountered in an everyday setting, would most likely stick out for all the wrong reasons. They will not be able to respond and emote in a way that makes sense to the observer. That is why the correct term for a sociopath is actually antisocial personality disorder (ASPD). The bottom line for a sociopath is that they cannot be motivated by the feelings of others, so the only natural motivator is their own desires. That means they will engage in any number of horrific acts because they have a disregard for societal norms and do not care about the emotional implications for others.

Sociopaths and psychopaths may have you thinking of serial killers, and you would not be wrong to do so. Serial killers are often diagnosed as suffering from mental illnesses that are ASPD or are associated with ASPD and psychopathy. You may recall that a serial killer has to have killed more than two people over a span of time. They are not like mass murderers who kill many in one large event or like a spree killer who kills multiple people over a shorter period of time. Serial killers can go through peaks and valleys throughout their killing careers and are often known to have "cooling off" periods that can last months or even years before they kill again.

A serial killer is most notable in dark psychology because of the extent to which they take their victimization. Dark psychology is about control, so, to a serial killer, the ultimate version of controlling a victim is murder. Once the victim is dead, the serial killer's control is complete. They may also enjoy the reactions of the victim because they lack empathy. In fact, the victim's reactions may provide them with a form of satisfaction or an emotional high that they cannot get in other circumstances.

Serial killers are also connected to narcissism and Machiavellianism. Serial killers would have a difficult time finding victims if they did not have the Dark Manipulation skills necessary to tempt victims to go with them or at least come near them. This is where Machiavellianism can come into play. The serial killer can fabricate carefully crafted lies that make the victim trust them or pity them. Then the victim's defenses are down, making it much easier for the serial killer to move forward with murdering them. Narcissism can be helpful for a serial killer because it can make them incredibly charming and self-assured. Confidence has its own kind of appeal, so a victim may find themselves believing in the trustworthiness of a serial killer wholeheartedly until it is too late. Both of these factors, as discussed before, can also be a downfall. Some notoriously narcissistic serial killers are so convinced of their own infallibility that they will try to represent themselves in court after they are caught. Their actual knowledge of the law plays no part in the decision because they are so convinced that they are too amazing to be outwitted by the justice system. They will adhere to the conviction that they are the best and deserve to be center stage, even if it means they risk being successfully prosecuted. This cockiness also means they can convince themselves that their lies are incredibly believable, but when someone comes along who is more self-aware, their lies can begin to unravel very quickly with a little careful scrutiny. That is why serial killers who are narcissists are often caught. The serial killers became so comfortable and predictable that it was only a matter of time before they were caught.

Another criminal label that can be difficult to understand but is still terrifying is an arsonist. An arsonist has a deep and abiding fascination with fire and the destruction it can cause., so they set fires to achieve an emotional high or some other kind of positive social return. They have a compulsion to set fires that can stem from any number of motivations or from seemingly no motivation at all.

We will first look at an arsonist who sets fires with a pre-existing motivation. These kinds of arsonists may be interested in revenge or may be interested in making themselves appear superior. They would fall on the Machiavellian corner of the Dark Triad. They have motives, they are methodical and thorough in their planning, and they will manipulate those around them to steer suspicion away from themselves. They also may be performative arsonists who are setting fires partially to gain information and partially to show off what they have done. They may even leave behind clues to taunt authorities or victims with the fact that they, the arsonist, have outwitted everyone else.

An arsonist who does not have a pre-existing motivation but who sets fires out of compulsion would more closely align with the psychopathic corner of the Dark Triad. There is a desire to act on impulse, to be chaotic, and to cause chaos. There is a complete disregard for consequences to others. They act with only the motivation to satisfy themselves and their need to create this chaos and destruction. In some ways, an arsonist resembles a sadist because they want to inflict a particular kind of pain, but they are often not directly motivated by hurting a particular victim.

Although arsonists have been included in this book, it is somewhat harder to make a case for how arsonists engage in dark psychology. There are victims of arson, yes, but the perpetrator is often less interested in the victims and more often fascinated by the fire and destruction of property. Whether or not people are victimized can be inconsequential. This is not always the case, and some arsonists do choose targets. However, they must be examined individually to determine whether or not dark psychology was a major, minor, or nonexistent contributor to the arsonist's actions. After all, an arsonist sets fires with the understanding that human victims may be involved. They understand this but set the fire anyway, so perhaps their victimization is that they do not care either way. If a fire creates a victim, that is of no consequence to the arsonist. The only goal is to start a fire.

Another criminal label that may stir some strong reactions is **terrorist**. A terrorist is someone who commits a violent or unlawful act that is designed to produce terror in the victims, often civilians, and is usually politically motivated. Terrorists are often aligned with an ideology that encourages them to engage in such acts frequently and with the design to create chaos and fear. These ideologies can have ties to governments, religions, or simply individuals who have created their own ideas around how the world should be. The acts of terror they commit are meant to cause a level of anarchy that will bring about the rise of their ideology and the fall of any opposing ideologies.

A terrorist has ties to dark psychology not so much because of what they do but because of why they do what they do. Behind most terrorists is an organization that is often headed by a leader. That terrorist leader is the key source of dark psychology. Similar to a cult leader, they will engage in any number of manipulation tactics to get their followers to perform terrorist acts. This includes brainwashing and mind games that are designed to break down the victim's previously held beliefs and coerce them into believing as the leader does. Then that victim becomes a new perpetrator. This means that the goal of the terrorist leader is to continually spawn new victims to become followers who then become perpetrators. This means that terrorist organizations may perhaps be more difficult to root out than some cults because the former victims who become perpetrators can learn to emulate the tactics used by their leaders and create mini-communities within the greater terrorist community. They replace their former susceptible personality with one that is manipulated into being by the leader. Once that transformation is complete, the victim has become a leader in their own way and is now free to perpetrate the same brainwashing and mind games on others in order to continue the cycle.

Terrorists can be closely aligned with psychopaths within the Dark Triad because they are invested in creating chaos, but the tactics they use are more Machiavellian in nature. The outcome is chaos and fear, but the plan was crafted methodically over time and was not an act of impulse. There is a dark design behind a terrorist organization. Otherwise, it would not be possible to continue to draw new members and turn them into new perpetrators. It is hard to say whether a terrorist can be said to lack empathy because they may be so brainwashed that they truly believe the crimes they commit are for the greater good. This does not and cannot excuse what they do, but it does beg the question of whether their free will was at play in the same way as someone who is not under the influence of a masterful Dark Manipulator. This also creates the conundrum of when or if the former victim, now perpetrator, has spent so long as a perpetrator that their previous role of victim becomes irrelevant. What is unclear is how to gauge when this line is crossed or whether the line exists at all. It is not clear cut, which is why terrorists are a difficult area of criminality to assess.

Another difficult criminal label to assess is a **sadist**. The sadist's goal is always the same, and that is to inflict some kind of pain or humiliation on someone else for the sake of satisfying the sadist's desires in some way. This falls squarely within the parameters of dark psychology. A sadist has no evolutionary motive for what they do. A sadist is always interested in victimizing. A sadist is also very interested in exacerbating and maximizing the dynamic between a victim and a perpetrator. They go beyond simply controlling the mind. They want their control to be so absolute that the victim's mind does not need to be controlled. The perpetrator has them so thoroughly within their power that they can inflict pain as they see fit. They manifest their control in an intense and readily apparent way. There is no question of whether the victim was exercising free will. The sadist's goal is to remove any kind of choice at all and leave the victim with only one option: pain.

It is important to note that a sadist differs from other kinds of deviant criminals because they are most interested in physical pain. Most other personality types and criminal types are also interested in psychological and emotional pain. A sadist will also enjoy this kind of pain, but the physical manifestation is definitely an important factor. What is also interesting about sadists is that they may be able to find willing victims. That sounds counterintuitive, but there are other kinds of people known as masochists who enjoy having pain inflicted on them. If a sadist is willing to take the time, they can seek out and find a masochist who will not only accept but enjoy the pain the sadist wants to inflict. Sometimes this scenario works out amicably, and both individuals are able to achieve the satisfaction they seek without there being any true victims. What they do is based on an agreement rather than coercion.

Sadists are most notable for the pleasure they derive from what they do. Watching others' pain is their pleasure, especially sexual pleasure. However, this means that many sadists will not be satisfied by inflicting pain on a masochist. Part of what gives them a thrill is the fact that their victim is not a willing participant in the pain. This is part of what increases their Dark Factor. They are disinterested in how others feel when pain is inflicted on them. The priority is the sadist's gratification at all times. This could be connected to egoism and/or narcissism. The sadist's needs and desires are the focal points, and the consequences to those around them are unimportant and trivial to the sadist. This is another label that many will find it hard to understand because they cannot understand why watching someone's fear, pain, and humiliation can create not just a sense of satisfaction but a sense of pleasure. This is not intended to shame those who engage in consensual acts with elements of sadism and/or masochism. Instead, it points to how a sadist's desire to inflict pain can take them further down the Dark Continuum and make it harder for others to understand their motivations and actions.

Another criminal label worth exploring is the **necrophile**. This is another label that is difficult to fathom as an average human being. A necrophile is someone who is attracted to corpses in a sexual way. This does not necessarily mean that these individuals intend to or have intercourse with corpses but rather that they are drawn to them and find the fact that they are dead sexually satisfying or arousing. There may also be some kind of spectrum within necrophilia because some individuals may be satisfied with the illusion that their victim is dead. This could be created by a drug-induced state or by some kind of role-playing scenario. There does not necessarily have to be a truly dead body for the necrophile to find gratification and enjoyment.

Now to examine how necrophilia may fit into the boundaries of dark psychology. Although a corpse is already dead, the argument could be made that a corpse is an ideal victim because they have no means to resist whatever acts are inflicted upon them by the necrophile. It is also an ideal setup for the perpetrator to have complete control over the victim in every way. However, necrophilia creates a very difficult situation when trying to analyze it from a dark psychological perspective. Although there is a perpetrator and there is a victim, the complication arises that the victim is dead. This means there is no mind to control nor actions to coerce. The other human being that the perpetrator is meant to have controlled is essentially no longer a human being once they are deceased. This begets the question of whether necrophiles should be considered a part of the Dark Continuum at all.

The undeniable connection between necrophilia and dark psychology is that it is often the case that the necrophile murdered the person that then becomes the corpse they are sexually attracted to. This is a definite example of extreme control and victimization. The perpetrator is so intent on reaching sexual gratification that they will use their control over the victim to first murder the victim and turn them into an attractive corpse. This is a very Machiavellian tendency because the manipulator is highly focused on one goal and will use any means to reach that goal.

The list of criminal labels could go on, but this is enough exposure to show you how dark psychology helps to illuminate what can make these criminals so successful in perpetrating their crimes. The power of the Dark Triad is undeniable, so when individuals engage in deviant behavior and also show dark personality traits, it is no wonder they become dangerous and often violent criminals. The narcissist, Machiavellian, and psychopath can all be at work alongside these other deviant criminal tendencies, which creates a Dark Factor that is incredibly strong. These Dark Manipulators can go to new and unknown places on the Dark Continuum, and it is possible that someday one of them will show us the true meaning of the Dark Singularity.

CHAPTER 9
Making Dark Psychology Work For You

You have finally made it nearly to the end of your journey into dark psychology and its many nuances. You will now have a thorough understanding of what it means to engage in dark psychology tactics and how the people around you may be using dark psychology to control and manipulate you. However, what is missing is how you can use dark psychology. After all, you are human, and every human has the capacity to engage in dark psychology. What this chapter aims to teach you is how you can take certain tactics and use them to create desirable outcomes for both you and the victim. This advice is not intended to encourage you to victimize others but rather to understand how dark psychology tactics can positively influence your life and do nothing negative to the "victim." In these scenarios, the "victim" is not being hurt by what you are doing. They may be giving you what you want because you used dark manipulation, but they will not be victimized by whatever you get out of the situation.

This section is not exhaustive, and it is always possible to go back through the text and discover another tactic you can reinvent to create positive effects. What you need to keep front of mind is that what you do is always done to induce good. As with the chapter on social media, question yourself about your motivations. Who does this benefit the most? What will be its short-term and long-term effects? Why do I want to do this? Will this encourage more positive developments for everyone involved? Will I be lying if I engage in this behavior? Each of these answers will let you see for yourself if you are straying too far down the Dark Continuum. That is the whole purpose of this book. The goal is to give you the power to understand yourself and those around you on a new level. You can now understand if your motivations are coming from a desire to do good or from a deeply human but possibly dark place within you where truly dark psychology lurks.

Revisiting Some Dark Tactics

In order to put you well on your way to practicing dark psychology, it is best to simply revisit some of the tactics discussed earlier, but this time to show how you can use those tactics to create positive outcomes for everyone involved. This may sound impossible or like it is a trap. That is not the point of these tips and tricks. They are meant to show how the victim can strike back and how the psychological and emotional push of dark psychology tactics can actually make the "victims" more fulfilled also. There is a way to lie on the lighter end of the Dark Continuum while still using dark psychology on a regular basis.

Choice Restriction

As you may recall from the chapter that explains some key terms, choice restriction is when a perpetrator provides a victim with choices but intentionally omits any choices the perpetrator finds undesirable. This is controlling because the victim is not a part of creating the choices and is duped into thinking they had a choice because multiple options were presented. It can be very misleading.

When you use choice restriction, what you are doing is limiting the "victim's" choices in such a way that helps the "victim" avoid making a mistake that may negatively impact both of your lives. For example, the "victim" could be your best friend who is deciding how to break up with an abusive partner and is now uncertain whether they want to break it off at all. As the perpetrator, you could tell them that they only have three choices, and within those three choices, you would only include scenarios that ended in the "victim" breaking up with their abusive partner. This is a positive way to use choice restriction because you are most interested in helping the "victim" rather than making them act in a way that is most beneficial to yourself.

Gift Giving

Gift giving can be manipulative when the gift giver's goal is to use the recipient's guilt to coerce them into doing a favor or returning the favor in a way that most benefits the giver. The perpetrator will often make the gift something large or very thoughtful in order to increase the likelihood that the victim will agree to do whatever the perpetrator desires.

When using gift giving positively, you are still going to give a gift that is thoughtful or large. This will still induce a sense of guilt in the "victim," but the goal or motivator should be to push the victim in a positive direction. For example, imagine that a family member has been neglecting to call and check on you even though you have recently fallen on hard times. In the past, you have always been there for them in similar situations and never failed to support them and check on them regularly. Rather than call them out for being neglectful, you can use the gift to remind them how hard you work to have a positive relationship with them, and this may push the "victim" to feel guilty enough to realize they have neglected you recently. This can save you an awkward conversation, and it can also help the "victim" regain some clarity about your relationship.

Guilt Inducement

Guilt inducement is similar in many ways to gift giving, except that it uses words instead of gifts to push the victim into taking action. Guilt inducement is the intentional use of statements or other behaviors to make a victim feel guilty for not being better to the perpetrator. These comments are often done passive-aggressively but are blatantly designed to make the victim feel such immense guilt that they may do any number of things to make the perpetrator feel better.

Guilt inducement can be an effective tool for positive change when used very carefully. Positive guilt inducement is best created through actions rather than through words because the "victim" may pick up on the passive-aggressive comments too easily. For example, imagine you have a sloppy roommate who was supposed to have cleared out the laundry room for you but instead has left their clothes strewn about and still in the dryer. Then, if the roommate asks you to go somewhere to some event, you can tell them you cannot. When the roommate asks you "why," you can respond that you have to wait until your clothes are washed because you do not have anything clean and appropriate to wear. You cannot, of course, make this comment sarcastically but, instead, have to show how sincerely sorry you are that you cannot make it. This should coerce the "victim" into realizing they were the reason you had to say no. It should also coerce them into finishing their chore so you can enjoy whatever event they wanted to attend. This creates positive outcomes for everyone.

Love Denial

Love denial is meant to make the victim miss the perpetrator's affection so much that they will do nearly anything to restore the perpetrator's displays of affection. This could mean the perpetrator does not touch the victim or refuses to participate in other outward shows of affection.

Love denial can be an effective tool in a relationship. This has to be a tactic that is not used frequently, and it must always be explained directly to the victim. For example, you could have a partner who has trouble listening to you when you have something truly serious to say to them. Perhaps you have already brought this topic several times before, but your partner still has not shown they recognize what you are trying to communicate. The next time the issue arises, you could begin using love denial. When your partner asks what is wrong, you then explain that you cannot show them affection until they show you an equal measure of affection by listening to what you have to communicate. They should be willing to take what you say more seriously when the stakes are so high. It is also an effective way to get your partner to pay attention when they may have become complacent in your relationship.

Love Flooding

Love flooding is the act of overwhelming someone with love and affection. It can be used to create a false sense of commitment and caring in a relationship. It can also lure a victim into believing that they are extremely important to the perpetrator, when, in fact, the perpetrator is only interested in how they can coerce the victim to behave as they desire.

It is also a misleading title because excessive compliments and other displays of affection do not necessarily equate to love.

Love flooding can be a positive choice in a relationship if your partner is perhaps becoming so comfortable in the relationship that they stop trying to show you how important you are to them. If you then flood them with love, you can remind them that your relationship goes beyond the trivial and is something special and separate from a mere friendship. Remind them through your love flooding that you cherish them and that your relationship is something that drives how you live your daily life. It is a chance for your partner to feel valued and appreciated again. This should be enough to shake them out of their stupor and guide them back to showering you with love and affection also. It can be a great way to rebook a relationship for both partners.

Priming

Priming is very subtle, and it may be a difficult skill to develop. Priming is the use of specific words or phrases along with related actions that encourage a person to have a particular response. These are subtle suggestions that get you primed to behave a certain way or have a certain response to a situation. You could think of priming as similar to grooming. Habits of thought are developed through carefully planted priming tactics.

Priming can be an excellent way to get someone to have a positive reaction to a request. For example, imagine you have a new project you want to present to your boss that really has the potential to make a large and lasting impact on the business. Rather than say that outright, you could prime your boss to have a positive response to your idea by dropping subtle hints about it in the weeks leading up to your presentation. Make little side comments on related topics or share a desirable development that would improve the company. When the boss hears your presentation, these subtle thoughts will creep back into their conscience and encourage them to hear your presentation with enthusiasm and encouragement. They may even feel like this is the idea they have been waiting for because your subtle hints all clearly led to this one central idea.

Reverse Psychology

Reverse psychology is an old tactic that you may already have used or have heard about so many times that you doubt its effectiveness. However, reverse psychology can still have a significant impact on someone's behavior. It is the conscious decision to encourage someone to act in a certain way that actually makes them do the opposite. That is the intent of the perpetrator all along. This is most effective when the victim is trying to strike back at the perpetrator in some way. They will do the opposite of what the perpetrator says out of a desire to deny them what they want.

Reverse psychology can have a positive effect when used carefully and in carefully chosen situations. For example, imagine that you have a friend who is angry at you for standing up to them when they treated a mutual friend poorly. What you could tell them is maybe they should just give up on your friendship if they want to act this way. The friend may respond that that is a good idea and act like they are going to leave you and end your friendship. What happens instead is that they will be so angry and so intent on not giving you what you want that they will begin arguing for your friendship and why you should stay friends. Now they are fighting for you to work through your differences rather than to allow the friendship to go through a falling out.

Withdrawal

Withdrawal can be a very dangerous action to take because it can so easily coerce a victim into inviting a perpetrator back into their lives because they "miss" them so much. It can be intensely manipulative because the victim will feel deprived of the perceived benefits they enjoyed while the perpetrator was still there.

Withdrawal can be an effective tool when a "victim" needs to see what the "perpetrator" is bringing to their relationship and relearn to appreciate the benefits of the relationship. Imagine you are in a romantic relationship, and your partner has begun to be obsessed with their career to the point that your relationship is always on hold because work comes first. However, your partner is still enjoying the benefits of your affection and attention without reciprocating. What you can do is first and foremost let them know you are withdrawing and why. Simply explain that you have noticed that they seem to need more time for their work and less time with you. You can present it as a way to help them get what they want. If they truly want to be dedicated so fully to work, then removing yourself from the picture should bring the "victim" closer to their desires. What it will do instead is show the "victim" how the "perpetrator" has been giving far more than they are receiving. This will encourage the "victim" to do what it takes to restore balance in the relationship so that both participants are actively engaged in developing together.

Leading Questions

Leading questions are designed to be a trap. The perpetrator will ask questions to which the victim has to respond yes. This allows the perpetrator to create a standard of response or behavior to which the victim must adhere in order to be consistent and stand by what they said. This is a common tactic among fundraisers. They will ask if you agree with a series of statements, perhaps about your commitment to helping the poor, and if you respond yes to every question, then it would seem unfeeling or contradictory to refuse to donate to a project that serves the very ideals you just verbally supported.

Leading questions can be a highly effective tool when you want to help guide someone to a logical conclusion without telling them directly what to do. For example, you may have a friend who is contemplating a career change from something more lucrative to something that is less lucrative but more fulfilling. You can ask a series of leading questions that help them see how feeling fulfilled is more important to them than money. This helps guide them to a decision that is more beneficial to them than it is to you.

Whether you choose to employ these tactics or not is your choice. Your study of dark psychology does not require that you practice dark psychology. These tactics are meant to give you a framework that will enable you to manipulate and coerce great things for yourself and, more importantly, for the people you care about. That is what will separate you from the other practitioners of dark psychology and keep you away from some of the darker topics we have covered in this book. Always ground your choices in a desire to do good for all rather than only to benefit yourself, and you will find yourself living in the light rather than the darkness.

As you revisit this toolkit, challenge yourself to look for new ways to make dark psychology work for you. You already have it in you, so why not use it to make your life better. Take control of your life back. Understand who and what is controlling your life now and how you lost control in the first place. Dark psychology can give you back what you lost and give you the confidence to step out into the world, knowing you are well-equipped to avoid being the victim.

CONCLUSION

Thank you for making it through to the end of *Dark Psychology Secrets*. The hope is that it gave you an understanding of the darkness that can infiltrate your life and seek to make you a victim. It is also meant to guide you to recognize those around you who may be using dark psychology to influence your life.

You first learned how to define dark psychology and understand its role in humanity. You then were able to explore the basic defining qualities of dark psychology, like the Dark Triad. After that, you learned an extensive number of terms that not only relate to dark psychology but also relate to other fields of study.

You now know what tactics are used by those who embrace dark psychology. You have the knowledge to see these tactics at work and to extricate yourself from their potentially negative influences. You also know who is more likely to engage in dark psychology simply by assessing their career choices and current occupation.

You are well-aware of how dark psychology can dig into the depths of evil in the form of deviant behavior and extremely dark individuals who have strayed closer and closer to the Dark Singularity. You can see how dark influences may lurk online when you open your social media accounts each day. You may have a fresh perspective on a famous criminal and how dark psychology changed the course of their criminal careers.

The next step is to take what you have learned and put it to use. You can now share it with others and help them discover how to avoid being the target of victimization. The point is that the choice is yours, and therefore the power is yours.

Finally, if you found this book useful in any way, be sure to leave a review on Amazon or recommend it to a friend.

DESCRIPTION

Have you ever wondered why you let yourself be guided and influenced by people you know are not good? Have you ever wanted to know how to avoid toxic relationships and manipulative people? Have you ever contemplated why certain people act the way they do? Have you ever felt your skin crawl because you knew someone was up to something, but you couldn't say what?

All of these questions can be answered with a quick study of the secrets of dark psychology. You no longer have to live in fear or doubt but will instead be equipped with all the tools you need to detect and deter dark forces that surround you on a daily basis. You will also begin to see how the darkness is all around you but is also avoidable. Your knowledge will expand in new and exciting ways as you dive deeper into dark psychology. In this book, you will discover:

- What dark psychology is
- The history behind the development of dark psychology as a field of study
- The characteristics that make dark psychology unique and also a menacing force
- The many complex terms associated with dark psychology and what they mean
- The methodology of dark psychology and how its tools can be used to terrible effect
- Who is most likely to use dark psychology and why
- Who has gone the deepest into the darkness and why
- How social media can be a powerful platform for practitioners of dark psychology
- The ways in which deviant behavior can be traced back to roots in dark psychology
- How to put dark psychology to use in your own life

All of this and more awaits you in *Dark Psychology Secrets*. It is an in-depth look at this field of study intended to make you an expert who is empowered and savvy.

Once you have read this book, you will be able to see the world from a totally new perspective. Each time you interact with someone, you will have a new sense of how their motivations could be influencing their actions. You will also have the power to see through their lies and tactics before you become their latest victim.

This book is also full of some of the important terms that are relevant to the study of this field. Instead of feeling inept or uninformed, you will become an authority on dark psychology. You will find others turning to you for guidance and information.

Dark Psychology Secrets is also for the curious who want to know more about the darker side of humanity. People are capable of horrific deeds, and dark psychology is the key to understanding how and why someone can engage in such monstrous acts. The possibilities are endless, and those who seek will find the answers in this book.

Finally, this text is the answer to how you prevent others from taking advantage of you. You will never again be steered by others but will rest easy knowing you have control of your own choices.

www.ingramcontent.com/pod-product-compliance
Lightning Source LLC
Chambersburg PA
CBHW071407070526
44578CB00002B/502